Indo-Russian Relations in the Post-Cold War Period (1991-2003)

Indo-Russian Relations in the Post-Cold War Period (1991-2003)

Anilkumar B Halu

AUTHORSPRESS
Publishers of Scholarly Books

Worldwide Circulation through Authorspress Global Network
First Published 2010
by
Authorspress
E-35/103, Jawahar Park
Laxmi Nagar, Delhi-110 092
e-mail: authorspress@yahoo.com

Indo-Russian Relations in the Post-Cold War Period (1991-2003)
ISBN 978-81-7273-552-4

Printed in India at Tarun Offset, Delhi.

Dedicated

To my father,

Shri Basavaraj Halu,

who showed me the power of Hard Work and Discipline.

To my mother,

Smt. Vijayalaxmi B. Halu,

whose love and silent support enriches my life.

Foreword

Dr. Anilkumar Halu, a hard working scholar did his M.Phil., and Ph.D. under my supervision from Gulbarga University, Gulbarga. Dr. Halu has many research papers to his credit which are published in many reputed journals and periodicals on international relations. His work on *"Indo-Russian Relations in the Post-Cold War Period (1991-2003)"* is most contemporary one and he deserves every encouragements.

The book deals with the bilateral relations of two important nations of the world during the post-cold war period. After the disintegration on of former Soviet Union, there was a kind of suspicion that the relations between India and Russia will take the U-turn. But, that was not the situation, rather the relations between there two nations further strengthened. The author in his book very well discussed various issues which dominated the scene after the end of cold war. Mr. V. Putin's period of Russian Presidency from 2000-2008 is regarded as landmarks in Indo-Russian Relations. During his period, bilateral talks were held with regular intervals and exchange of visits by both Heads of Governments and Heads of States of the two countries increased and during these official visits, agreements were signed on various issues.

Former Soviet Union was the regular supplier of modern weapons and other military materials. The successor state of Russia is also following the same path. Recently, India and Russia are trying to form a strategic triangle with China. China being a emerging important power, having closer relations with that nation is in the interest of all the three nations. But, the efforts in this regard are very slow and the expected result is not been seen yet.

Lastly, I congratulate Dr. Anilkumar Halu, for his painstaking effort who dealt with the important subject of bilateral relations. He has tried his level best to put forth his ideas before the scholars, teachers and even the common people. I am sure that, it will be a useful addition to the existing literature on Indo-Russian Relations in particular and International Relations in general.

Gulbarga

Dr. Chandrakant Yatanoor
Professor,
Dept. of Political Science,
Gulbarga University,
Gulbarga
Karnataka-India.

Preface

Indo-Russian relations are civilisational and time-tested. These have traditionally been based on continuity, trust and mutual understanding. The importance attached to them cuts across party lines in India and is not subject to political vicissitudes. There is a national consensus on the need for a strong and stable relationship with the Russian Federation. A similar consensus exists in Russia on close and friendly ties with India. This is no mere rhetoric because India has received, earlier from the Soviet Union and thereafter from its successor state Russia, extremely valuable political, diplomatic and strategic support on vital issues affecting India's national interests. At crucial times, it was this country that consistently stood by us in international forums on vital issues like Kashmir and other matters affecting out territorial integrity and sovereignty. It was Soviet diplomatic backing and material support, and the confidence provided by the Indo-Soviet Treaty of Peace, Friendship and Cooperation, which enabled us to successfully undertake the Bangladesh operations in 1971.

With the focus of public attention on the foreign policy front over the last year or so having been on India's relations with the United States, it is easy to miss the significance of our bilateral relations with Russia. But it is important for the people of India to be aware of the importance of the relationship with Russia because, it is as close as it comes to being a true strategic partnership, yet one about which the general public remains somewhat ignorant. In the absence of widespread people-to-people contacts (trade, economic projects in the private sector, flow of tourists and students, a large and influential Indian diaspora), and given the handicaps of language, Russia does not affect most ordinary people's lives as does, say, the US or the Gulf region. At the Government level, however, over the years successive Indian leaders have taken special care to nurture this relationships, which has survived political vicissitudes, neglect and drift during the Yeltsin era, pressures and attempts by outside powers to create rifts, and occasional misunderstandings over Pakistan. On relations with Russia there is a consensus across the entire Indian political establishment.

As the Soviet Union broke-up, the whole edifice of trade and economic relations built up over decades came crashing down. Both sides scrambled to adjust to the new realities because it was inescapable. Political relations too reached a nadir during the Yeltsin era because the Russian leadership was too obsessed with the West and did not consider relations with India a sufficiently important priority. At a time when India-Russia relations were at an important crossroads, it was then Russian President Vladimir Putin who revived and steered the relationship in the right direction. From floundering phase of post-soviet chaos, India and Russia have found enough reasons to season their bilateral contacts with salt and pepper of national interests. The forward march of this long journey is laden with evidences and crimson hopes for a better tomorrow, hopefully yet to come in the years ahead.

Hence, the book is an effort to analyse the Indo-Russian relations in its varied facets during the post-cold war period and surely, it would stand to benefit students, scholars, diplomats, academics and all those interested in studying India, Russia and their mutual interests in the modern world.

Dr. Anilkumar Halu

Acknowledgements

It is my utmost pleasure to express my gratitude and very thanks to my advisor Dr. Chandrakant Yatanoor, professor of Political Science Department,. Gulbarga University, Gulbarga for his constant guidance, patience and encouragement. This work has gained immensely from his meticulous scrutiny and vital observations, without his help it would not have been possible to give this work the present shape. I gratefully acknowledge the support and encouragement he gave in completing this study.

I thank my parents, parents-in-laws, my brothers and sister for much empathy and loving solicitude and encouragements. Always being my side I owe them a great deal for their tremendous moral support they extended to me while I worked on the study.

I owe a lot to my wife Suhasini, as her encouragement, patience, emotional support and willingness to help in the completion of this book.

I offer thanks to my trusted friend and mentor, Prof. A Shivakanth Shetty for his generosity, optimism, faith and superb guidance.

Last but not least, I would like to express my sincere gratitude to Authorespress publishers for bringing out his book.

Needless to say the responsibility for any remaining errors and shortcomings in this book rest with me.

Dr. Anilkumar Halu

//

Contents

1

Indo-Soviet Relations during the Cold War Period

Introduction

The Indo-Russian relations have traditionally been marked by a remarkable degree of continuity and stability, based on national consensus in countries, as well as mutual goodwill and trust and sensitivity to mutual interests and concerns. The Indo-Russian relations are time-tested and based on continuity, trust and mutual understanding. It is comprehensive and multifaceted, and encompasses all areas including political, economic, defence, scientific and technological and cultural spheres, based on shared perceptions and mutuality of interests and mutual benefit.

After the disintegration of USSR and the emergence of Russia as an independent State in 1991 Russia declared itself to be State-continuator of the erstwhile USSR. India recognised Russia as the successor State to the former Soviet Union. The Russian leadership has described Russia's relations with India as being "special."[1]

Former President Boris Yeltsin in his public references to India mentioned continuing traditionally friendly relations and cooperation with India. Relations with Russia are an important foreign policy priority for India too. The need for close relations with India has also been referred by President Vladimir Putin who has stressed the geopolitical significance of the Indo-Russian relations. In the Foreign Policy concept released by the Russian Federation on July 10, 2000, it has been stated that, one of the crucial directions in the Russian foreign policy in Asia is to maintain friendly relations with the leading Asian states, including India. There is however speculation in some circle both in Russia and India that these good relations may suffer a setback because of the changes taking place in the former Soviet Union, in eastern Europe as well as in India.[2]

What is the significance of the Indo-Russian relations in the emerging foreign policy dynamics of India? First of all, the absence of the cold war has created a perfect atmosphere for India to pursue strategic partnership with both the US and Russia. Secondly, Indian and Russian leaderships have convergent views on several critical foreign policy issues, such as terrorism, US intervention in Iraq, and Iranian nuclear question. In all these issues New Delhi and Washington do not hold similar views, whereas Russian and Indian positions are strikingly similar. Yet, the Bush Administration holds nothing against India, unlike such situations during the cold war days. Thirdly, Russia is fast emerging as an energy superpower. This new role of Russia in sustaining energy security has coincided with India's growth as an economic power house, whose demand for energy will keep on rising in the foreseeable future. This is an area where the Russia-India cooperative engagement is going to be particularly crucial. Fourthly, Russia has proven itself to be a reliable defence and technology supplier. Although, India is seeking more advanced technology than Russia can possibly offer in certain sectors, there are a host of areas where Russian technology would be more appropriate for Indian situations. One such area is nuclear technology. Significantly, Russia has come forward with the offer of reactors at a time when India and the US are still struggling to conclude the 123 agreement to facilitate trade in civilian nuclear technology.

It appears that India's engagement had considerably slowed down over the years. Before late, the pace of bilateral engagement with Russia needs to be quickly enhanced. Vladimir Putin's visit to India in 2002 has set the new ball rolling and India needs to carry it forward. Russia is a powerful actor in international politics. Developments in Iraq, Iran and North Korea have contributed to the return of the Great Bear as a significant global player. Three critical foreign policy issues present an opportunity for India and Russia to come together to address such issues for mutual benefits. First, the need for creating a multipolar global structure has never been more required. Unipolarity has led to unilateral actions by the only superpower, which in turn has hurt everybody's interest. Careful coordination of policy among major powers can create a political balance not military to prevent unilateralism. Secondly, the non-military security threats in Eurasia, such as drug trafficking, religious extremism and terrorism make it imperative for a closer Russo-Indian cooperation. Finally, Russia can be an ally in ensuring energy security for India. The splendour in the current geo-economic and geopolitical scenario lies in the fact that India annoys none when it seeks to improve ties with Russia. In this context, it is very important and useful to conduct research on the problems and prospects of Indo– Russian relations during the post-cold war period.

History of Indo-Russian Relations

Soviet Union came into existence in 1917 as a result of the Russian Revolution based on Marxian-Socialist ideology. In accordance with the socialist ideology, right from the beginning, the Soviet Union condemned colonialism and supported freedom struggles including that of India. The process of planning adopted by the Soviet Union made it a developed and a powerful State within a few years. India's leaders fighting against British imperialism, and facing the consequences of capitalist oppression were obviously appreciative of both the Soviet support for its freedom struggle and the achievements that country had made. They, therefore, did not share Western countries' apprehensions about communist expansionist designs.

Pre-Cold War Period

At the time of independence, the expectation was for development of relationship of cooperation between the two countries, irrespective of differences of ideologies. Hope was strengthened with the Soviet Union formally recognising India as a sovereign State in April 1947, that is, four months before its independence, and establishment of diplomatic relations. However, at the time of India's independence the Soviet Union was under the control of Stalin, who was very rigid in his approach which included the perception that all those who were not communists were against the Soviet Union. India's joining the Commonwealth after independence was projected as India's pro-Western policy.[3] Similarly, India's adoption of non-alignment and its independent stand on certain issues at that time did not please Soviet Union.

As such, in 1947, the Soviet Union was quite sceptical about India's independence and its future identity. The situation, however, started changing from 1953 onwards. With the end of the Stalin era, a new Soviet leadership the began to look towards the newly independent Afro-Asian countries as its natural allies. It, therefore, appreciated India's non-alignment. The Soviet leadership realised that India was not suffering from any perceived threat of the spread of communism. In fact, India was resisting the expansion of Western influence into Asian region if it threatened self-determination. India had adopted a policy of non-alignment to address its own security and national concerns. Above all, the Soviet Union realised India's importance as a strategic partner when in 1954 Pakistan joined SEATO and CENTO alliances, and provided a basis to America on Russian borders. As a consequence, the Soviet Union considered Pakistan as an American client State, advancing and nurturing the US military and strategic interests in the region. From this period onwards relations between India and the Soviet Union started developing very cordially and friendly. One area in which Soviet Union has solidly stood by India was in regard to Kashmir. By 1955 it had clearly taken a pro-India stand and declared unequivocally that Jammu and Kashmir was an integral part of India. As has already been mentioned above in the discussion on Indo-US relations, some other events in international arena and country's responses to them further brought the Soviet Union and India closer vis-à-vis Pakistan and the USA.[4]

Along with strategic relations, gates were opened for trade and economic relations. The beginning was made with the Indo-Soviet Trade Agreement of 1953. It was followed by another agreement in 1955 for the construction of Bhilai Steel Plant. India received economic aid from the Soviet Union at low interest rates and on a long-term basis. An important aspect of trade relations has been the rupee trade. It means that trade was regulated under the rupee agreement under which imports into India were to be paid through export commodities. Transactions involving free foreign exchange were eliminated and the rupee served as an account unit. The trade relations between India and the USSR developed enormously. During the cold war, India's goal was to avoid being drawn into the sphere of influence of the major superpowers. At the same time, India required weapons for its defence, especially after the Chinese aggression in 1962. Indian defence procurement was limited due to budgetary constraints and a scarcity of foreign exchange. Under pressure from Pakistan and for its own strategic reasons, the United State provided only limited weapons, that too under conditions prevailing immediately after Chinese aggression. But the Soviet equipment was sold to India on concessional rates and lower rates of interest, and on long-term schedules. During India's war with China, the Soviet Union generally supported India's position. During India-Pakistan war in 1965, Pakistan freely used American weapons, their sophisticated tanks and some of the Chinese weapons against India. Further, the United States' efforts to come closer to China and possibilities of US-China-Pakistan axis were also a matter of serious concern for India.[5]

The impact of the US-China-Pak axis became clear during the Bangladesh crisis in 1971. It was in this situation that in August 1971 a Treaty of Peace, Friendship and Cooperation was signed between India and the erstwhile Soviet Union. This treaty proved to be a deterrent and the USA did not intervene in the war. The 1971 Treaty was the first political treaty concluded by India with one of the superpowers. Many critics observed that it was a deviation from non-alignment, but given the situation and America's direct threat, perhaps it was essential. In India the treaty was universally hailed. Hence, onwards the Indo-Soviet relations continued to develop under all governments in India. So much so that, even at the time of clear indications of the collapse of the Soviet Union, the 1971 Treaty, which was signed for 20 years, was renewed for another two decades in August 1991. In general, India-Soviet Union relations were based on mutual benefit and certain common visions about international politics. Both believed in national freedom and social equality, support to national liberation movements and fight against colonialism, racial discrimination and oppression as a matter of principle. Of course, the military and strategic interests of both the countries played a pivotal role in determining these relations. The same in many ways still continues as the India-Russia relations.[6]

Post-Cold War Period

The disintegration of the Soviet Union and the end of the cold war has brought about a fundamental transformation in the geopolitical map of the world.[7] The most prominent among the successor states of the Soviet Union, Russia, in spite of inheriting the formidable military might of its predecessor, suddenly found it reduced to the position of a second-ranking or regional power. Its predicament was further compounded by economic chaos and political uncertainty at the domestic level. The new leaders of Russia besieged by domestic constraints were not immediately in a position to clearly define the foreign policy goals of their state and ascertain its position in the emerging post-cold war international order. It was clearly pulled between a declining nostalgia for past relations with countries like India and growing proclivity towards cultivating relations with the West.[8] The first couple of years of India's relations with post-Soviet Russia were marked by a good deal of uncertainty, inconsistency and lack of clarity.

India did take early steps, though without making any significant headway. The two-track approach that it adopted was on the one hand aimed at resurrecting the vital elements of its economic and military relations with Russia and on the other, searching out alternatives in the West. On both these counts, however, its efforts were rewarded to a limited extent. Its difficulties were compounded both by the magnitude of its dependence on Russia and the political-economic uncertainty faced by the latter. It meant that it often had to 'wait and see' what Russia would do and how this would effect the relationship of the two countries.[9] However, Russia seems to have shredded its initial hesitation, inconsistency and unclarity. The contours of the new Russian foreign policy have become clearer. It is now giving all the indications of its ability and intentions of redefining its foreign policy goals, priorities and international role. With India the objectives and character of its relations are being defined with a measure of clarity. The national goals of the two countries are being looked upon in the light of new international realities. The two countries have once again begun to rediscover the mutual importance but with a qualitative difference, which commensurates with the realities of the post-cold war era.

The Indo-Russian cooperation in the area of defence supplies is gaining momentum. The Indo-Russian defence supplies are in the range of 70 per cent of the total defence imports of India. Agreements on scientific collaboration between India and Russia in the area of biotechnology have begun a new phase. Agreements have been signed for the Mig 29 K fighter, Kamov 31 helicopters, T 90S tanks and other defence equipment. Nearly $ 3 billion defence contracts have been finalised. Indian Navy has acquired two submarines and three frigates from Russia, which costs around $ 300 million each. The Navy is also acquiring three Krivak-class frigates or project 1135.6 from Russia. There are some indicators which show that Indo-Russian cooperation in the peaceful use of nuclear technology, related particularly to nuclear energy have already taken concrete shape. In the oil and gas sector, the Gas Authority of India Ltd. and Russia's Gazprom have signed a contract in the field of oil exploration.[10] The Indo-Russian politico-strategic defence cooperation is an important element of strategic partnership between the two countries.

Since both the countries are struggling to define their relations with other major players on the global stage, in a situation where the rules of international politics are in a state of flux and where the term of the economic interaction between nations are being reset, this specific encounter between the Indian and Russian leaderships was of significance for the affirmation of continuity and mutual reassurance that it symbolised.[11] What has substance to it is the reinforcement of the faith. There is a real convergence of perspectives on issues as wide-ranging as the phenomenon of terrorism, ensuring the security of nuclear weapons stockpiles in a world facing a new assortment of threats and challenges, the conservation and promotion of multi-polarity in global politics.

Between Vladimir Putin's first visit to India as president of Russian Federation in October 2000 and his second visit in December 2002, the framework for India-Russia relations was firmly set.[12] This was a framework of another special relationship of strategic partnership, expanding cooperation and multiplying contacts in various fields, some of them of critical importance to India-Russia both. What was different and special to this special relationship was that it was not born out of any cold war considerations nor was it either seemingly or even indirectly directed against any other country. It did not exclude the establishment of other special relationships provide they were not inimical to either of them. It reflected the changed and changing international situation and their mutual needs and requirements. Above all, it reflected the fact that not only there were no national irritants but that there was an obvious long-term complementarily of interests between the two countries.

Undoubtedly, both India and Russia are sovereign countries and would be looking after their own in the first instance. The understanding between Russia and India flowed from the complimentarily of their interests both in historical, geopolitical and futuristic terms. Whether it was the question of terrorism or of the defence of Indian territorial integrity or that of Russia, whether it was a question of India's role in this region and the world and on most international issues of importance to the two countries, the Russian and Indian interests generally tended to coincide and there is a certain empathy for each other.[13] There is therefore, an intrinsic value in the Indo-Russia ties. This does not exclude differences of approach on certain specific issues, but the general, overall parallelism of interests has been evident. The two sides so far have soft understanding of each other's concerns while retaining their autonomy of action and expanding their relations with diverse other countries.

The Indo-Russian relations remained smooth and continuous though they have gone through distinct phases in their history and development.[14] Interestingly, these phases relate to the national interests of these two countries as well as each of these phases have some relation to the global situation. One can classify these phases as 1947-1956, 1956-1971, 1971-1985, 1985-1996 and 1996 onwards. In each of these phases the Indo-Russian relations have grown or declined depending on the perceptions and experiences that both the countries have had mainly with the Western powers. The rough period in Russian-Indian relations after 1985 clearly arose from the felt need of both to connect more seriously with the West. The restabilisation of relations between the two after 1996 materialised again when both Russia and India experienced that the West, especially the United States, did not live up to their expectations to deliver its promises to both these countries.

Each of these phases has some distinct characteristics in terms of trade and political relations. For instance, in phase 1956-1971 and 1971-1985 trade between the two was state dominated but this ended after phase 1985-1996. From phase 1996 onwards trade has dominated by military hardware and joints military production between the two sides. There is a fundamental base line in the relation between these two countries that has built up over the years. This base involves India's dependence on military hardware imports from Russia, political support on its position on Kashmir and other economic, cultural and political links as also no real antagonism on any major issues. Currently both countries find themselves on similar platform on issues ranging from terrorism, impact of globalisation, Iraq, etc. There is thus a common vision between the two countries that seems to be re-emerging as the test of bilateral ties lies in the commonality of approach to problems and conflicts.

The post-cold war world has become, to borrow Samuel Huntington's phrase, 'a multi-polar and multi-civilisational' entity. Russia, shrunk from its Soviet Union size, is trying to carve out a new role for itself. Right from the time of the Czars, it has been craving for a substantial niche in the European scene. However, it remained more or less cut off from the West and gradually came to be seen as an 'Eastern' power.

India's strategic contact with Russia began only after independence. Though, the British colonial rulers did periodically raise the bogey of Russia's southward expansion towards the Indian Ocean, it remained more or less in realms of conjecture. The former Soviet Union not only became India's strategically – albeit an informal one – vis-a-vis the West-supported Pakistan, but also an inspiration for our planned economic development. The trade ties too became very strong.

The post-Soviet era Russian worldview became Euro-centric. This, combined with the economic chaos within the country, resulted in jeopardising its commercial ties with developing countries and in placing the Indo-Russian relations on the backburner. However, the Russians were soon disillusioned with the West and hastened to mend fences with India and other Asian neighbours. Even though Russia gives more importance to China and Japan, India remains a potentially crucial partner for Russia, which the latter appears now to be trying to rediscover. Moreover, China has emerged a strong partner of Russia and it is felt that their relationship might culminate in an alliance. This might adversely affect the Indo-Russian equation, especially if the Sino-Indian relations deteriorate. Here, one would like to add that China has been the backbone of Pakistan's military build-up – something that New Delhi is unlikely to forget in a hurry. Sooner or later this issue will become a bone of contention between the two Asian giants.

Russia learned the hard way that there are no free lunches in international relations and wants to conduct its foreign relations for its own economic advantages. Moscow feels disturbed at the changing attitude of India supported by its enlarged purse from privatisation and liberalisation of its economy. As a stable ally of India during the so-called cold war era, the then USSR under N.Khrushchev adopted a pro-India stance since 1950s with a view to restraining the US influence in the region and the developing world at large and voluntarily assisted the Indian projects for self-reliance in core industries with means and technology as well as specialists from the Soviet side. Continued large scale material support to the Third World, however, became a big burden on the Soviet Union spending huge resources to contain the US political aggressions and the freedom struggles the world over.

New Delhi has long ago realised that Moscow could not be "exploited" and used for its own benefits, as before, by making common ground the issues of Kashmir and Chechnya or terrorism plank. For Moscow, India is just one of the countries in Asia with which Russia has been keen to increase the trade volume. Putin's visits, though encouraged the ties to develop without much jerks, yet failed to enhance the bilateral ties as it was the case during the Soviet era. India's longing for the West, especially the USA and Israel for weapons and technology as well other world privileges, made things worse for the Russo-Indian relations and, therefore, the ties have not been conducted quite as satisfactorily, as it should have been. The end of the cold war also caused a cold relationship of Russia with a host of its former allies and friends, including India. With the de-ideologisation of Soviet politics initiated during the M. Gorbachev era for bringing USSR closer to the Western civilisation and world markets, made Moscow revitalise its shaken economy. It was not until the visit of former Russian President Boris Yeltsin, after a long wait, in 1999 a new hope was generated in Indo-Russian relations. Totally disillusioned with the fate of his pro-West policies, Yeltsin began turning to Eurasian countries by 1996 for special focus of ties. When he visited India the media projected the trip as historical, but the results showed that expectations were shortlived, as Russia now was keen to enter into agreements with developing world, India inclusive, for mutual benefits and not for India's cause alone any more. But it cannot be denied that there is an enormous legacy of multifaceted relationship and vast reservoir of goodwill between the two countries, which can help promote mutually beneficial commercial and strategic ties. Therefore, the present study makes an attempt to probe the Indo-Russian relations during the post cold war period under the changed circumstances.

It is indeed a Herculean task to understand and analyse the complex but inevitable issues and problems that we are facing today in the post-cold war period. There is a general consensus among scholars and policy practioners that in view of the end of cold war politics, and demise of the communist Soviet Union, there is a categorical need to think afresh the issues the divide and unite the humankind. Keeping this profound dilemma, the present study makes an honest attempt to make a dispassionate explorations into complex issues such as post cold war military doctrines and disarmament, WTO, and Third World concerns, challenges and opportunities lying before the political, strategic, cultural, trade and military hobnobbing between India and Russia and their impact on the new world order. Though, there are studies available by academics, and economists, both Indian and Russian dealing with the Indo–Russian relations from various angles. In this study, however, an attempt has been made to analyse the Indo–Russian relations in the new historical conditions after the end of the cold war in which the entire thought structure of Russia is undergoing a basic transformation in which India has lot of stakes.

Moreover, the present study will be of value not only to those who wish to understand the new direction of the Indo– Russian relations but also to academics, diplomats and, above all, to those who aspire to build meaningful ties with the Russia. This comprehensive study in this sense would serve the requirements of all sections of the concerned people of our country.

This study on India's relations with Russia and China in the post-cold war period based on empirical studies in the end of the present century is of far reaching importance both for Indian and foreign experts. These three countries have a large number of common problems. Therefore, strengthening of their political, economic, and cultural relations through interaction with each other has its own significance. The centre of gravity of the world power in the end of the present century has already shifted from Europe to the Asia-Pacific region. The United States, China, Japan and Russia are already engaged in a power struggle in this region. In the beginning of the next century, Southeast Asia and India are likely to play an important role. Seen in this context the relations among these three nations in the coming decades will play a decisive role in this region. Nevertheless, it will be simplistic to conclude that these countries are moving in a direction of forming an alliance. The crux of the problem is to analyse objectively bilateral and trilateral relations among these three countries. This study makes a valuable contribution in theory of international relations.

References

1. Dash, P.L. 'Soviet Disintegration and Challengers in Indo-CIS Relations' in Stephen P Cohen, Ed 'South Asia After the Cold War: International Perspectives: ACDIS Papers. New York, 1992 p.5.
2. Ibid.p.7.
3. Nivedita Das Kundu, on "Indo-Russian Relations: An Overview", available at http://www.helsinki.fi/aleksanteri/english/publications/ ap_das_kundu.htm, Also See Jasjit Singh, Trends in Defence Expenditure, *Asian Strategic Review* 1998-99, p. 28.
4. Jerome M Conley, 'India-Russia Military and Nuclear Cooperation: Implications for US Security.' US Air Force, National Strategic Institute Studies Paper, February 2000, p. 87.
5. Shelton U. Kodikara, 'South Asian Security Dilemmas in the Post-Cold War World' in Stephen P Cohen, Ed, ACDIS Papers, New York, 1992 quoted above. p 149.
6. Dixit, J.N. 'Across Borders: Fifty Years of India's Foreign Policy', New Delhi, Picus Books, 1998 p.180.
7. Jyotsna Bakshi, advanced her argument on Russia's Post-Pokhran Dilemma, *Strategic Analysis,* August 1998.p.65
8. Roy Medvedev, Vladimir Putin, New Accents in Russia's Foreign Policy, *Rossiskaya Gazeta,* August 8,2000.p.32
9. Michael Mandelbaum, Ed., *The New Russian Foreign Policy, A Council of Foreign Relations Book,* Brookings Institute, New York, 1998, pp. 13-14.
10. Nivedita Das Kundu, op. cit., pp. 40-47.
11. News From Russia, *Weekly News Bulletin* Edited and Published by the Information Department of the Russian Embassy in India, Issue No. 39, dated 27th Sept. 2002.
12. *Ria Novosti,* May 31, 2002.
13. *The Current Digest of the Post-Soviet Press,* February 4, 1998, 50 (1), pp. 1-2.
14. Lounev, Russia and India Political Cooperation in the sphere of Global regional and Bilateral Relations, *China Report* 381, 2002, pp.109-111.

2

Resurgence of Russia in the New Millennium (After 1991)

Introduction

With the dissolution of the Soviet Union in December 1991, the Republic of the Russian Federation become an independent country. Russia was the largest of the fifteen Republics that made up the Soviet Union, accounting for over 60 per cent of the GDP and over half of the Soviet population. The Russians also dominated the Soviet military and the Communist Party. Thus, Russia was widely accepted as the Soviet Union's successor state in diplomatic affairs and it assumed the USSR's permanent membership and veto in the UN Security Council.

Despite this acceptance, post-Soviet Russia lacked the military and political power of the former USSR. Russia managed to make the other ex-Soviet republics voluntarily disarm themselves of nuclear weapons and concentrated them under the command of the still effective rocket and space forces, but for the most part the Russian army and fleet were in near disarray by 1992. Prior to the dissolution of the Soviet Union, Boris Yeltsin had been elected President of Russia in June 1991 in the first direct presidential election in Russian history. In October 1991, as Russia was on the verge of independence, Yeltsin announced that Russia would proceed with radical market-oriented reform along the lines of Poland's "big bang,"[1] also known as "shock therapy."[2] Russia today shares many, continuities of political culture and social structure with its Tsarist and Soviet past.

DISMANTLING OF COMMUNISM IN USSR

The programmes of liberalisation and stabilisation were designed by Yeltsin's Deputy Prime Minister Yegor Gaidar, a 35-year-old liberal economist inclined toward radical reform, and widely known as an advocate of "shock therapy".[3] Shock therapy began days after the dissolution of the Soviet Union, when on January 2, 1992, Russian President Boris Yeltsin ordered the liberalisation of foreign trade, prices and currency. This entailed removing Soviet-era price controls in order to lure goods back into under stocked Russian stores, removing legal barriers to private trade and manufacture, and cutting subsidies to state farms and industries while allowing foreign imports into the Russian market in order to break the power of state-owned local monopolies. The partial results of liberalisation (lifting price controls) included worsening already apparent hyperinflation (after the Central Bank, an organ under parliament, which was sceptical of Yeltsin's reforms, was short of revenue and printed money to finance its debt) and the near bankruptcy of much of Russian industry.

The process of liberalisation would create winners and losers, depending on how particular industries, classes, age groups, ethnic groups, regions, and other sectors of Russian society were positioned. Some would benefit by the opening of competition; others would suffer. Among the winners were the new class of entrepreneurs and black marketeers that had emerged under Mikhail Gorbachev's *perestroika*. But liberalising prices meant that the elderly and others on fixed incomes would suffer a severe drop in living standards, and people would see a lifetime of savings wiped out.

With inflation at double-digit rates per month as a result of printing, macroeconomic stabilisation was enacted to curb this trend. Stabilisation, also called structural adjustment, is a harsh austerity regime (tight monetary policy and fiscal policy) for the economy in which the government seeks to control inflation. Under the stabilisation programme, the government let most prices float, raised interest rates to record highs, raised heavy new taxes, sharply cut back on government subsidies to industry and construction, and made massive cuts in state welfare spending. These policies caused widespread hardship as many state enterprises found themselves without orders or financing. A deep credit crunch shut down many industries and brought about a protracted depression.

The rationale of the programme was to squeeze the built-in inflationary pressure out of the economy so that producers would begin making sensible decisions about production, pricing and investment instead of chronically overusing resources-a problem that resulted in shortages of consumer goods in the Soviet Union in the 1980s. By letting the market rather than central planners determine prices, product mixes, output levels, and the like, the reformers intended to create an incentive structure in the economy where efficiency and risk would be rewarded and waste and carelessness were punished. Removing the causes of chronic inflation, the reform architects argued, was a precondition for all other reforms: hyperinflation would wreck both democracy and economic progress, they argued; they also argued that only by stabilising the state budget could the government proceed to dismantle the Soviet planned economy and create a new capitalist Russia.[4]

Obstacles to Capitalist Reform in Russia

A major reason that Russia's transition has been so wrenching is that the country is remaking both its Soviet-era political and economic institutions at once. In addition, Russia is also remaking itself as a new national state following the disintegration of the union. The former Soviet Union was dealt a number of unique obstacles during the post-Soviet transition. These obstacles may have left Russia on a far worse footing than other former Communist-led states to Russia's west that were also going through dual economic and political transitions, such as Poland, Hungary and the Czech Republic, which have fared better since the collapse of the Eastern bloc between 1989 and 1991.

The first major problem facing Russia was the legacy of the Soviet Union's enormous commitment to the cold war. In the late 1980s, the Soviet Union devoted a quarter of its gross economic output to the defence sector (at the time most Western analysts believed that this figure was 15 per cent).[5] At the time, the military-industrial complex employed at least one of every five adults in the Soviet Union. In some regions of Russia, at least half of the workforce was employed in defense plants. (The comparable US figures were roughly one-sixteenth of gross national product and about one of every sixteen in the workforce.) The end of the cold war and the cutback in military spending hit such plants very hard, and it was often impossible for them to quickly retool equipment, retrain workers, and find new markets to adjust to the new post-cold war and post-Soviet era. In the process of conversion an enormous body of experience, qualified specialists and knowhow has been lost, as the plants were sometimes switching from producing hi-tech military equipment to making kitchen utensils.

A second obstacle, partly related to the sheer vastness and geographical diversity of the Russian landmass, was the sizable number of "mono-industrial"[6] regional economies (regions dominated by a single industrial employer) that Russia inherited from the Soviet Union. The concentration of production in a relatively small number of big state enterprises meant that many local governments were entirely dependent on the economic health of a single employer; when the Soviet Union collapsed and the economic ties between Soviet republics and even regions were severed, the production in the whole country dropped by more than fifty percent. Roughly half of Russia's cities had only one large industrial enterprise, and three-fourths had no more than four. Consequently, the decrease in production caused tremendous unemployment and underemployment.

Thirdly, post-Soviet Russia did not inherit a system of state social security and welfare from the USSR. Instead, the companies, mainly large industrial firms, were traditionally responsible for a broad range of social welfare functions—building and maintaining housing for their workforces, and managing health, recreational, educational and similar facilities. The towns in contrast possessed neither the apparatus nor the funds for the provision of basic social services. Industrial employers were left heavily dependent on their firms. Thus, economic transformation created severe problems in maintaining social welfare since local governments were unable to assume financial responsibilities for these function.

Finally, there is a human capital dimension to the failure of post-Soviet reforms in Russia. The former Soviet population was not necessarily uneducated. Literacy was nearly universal, and the educational level of the Soviet population was among the highest in the world with respect to science, engineering, and some technical disciplines. But the Soviets devoted little to what would be described as "liberal arts" in the West.[7] The former Soviet Union's state enterprise managers were indeed highly skilled at coping with the demands on them under the Soviet system of planned production targets. But the incentive system built into state institutions and industries during the Soviet era encouraged skill in coping with state-run planned economy, but discouraged the risk-and-reward centred behaviour of market capitalism. For example, the directors of Soviet state firms were rewarded for meeting output targets under difficult conditions, such as uncertainty about whether needed inputs would be delivered in time and in the right assortment. As noted, they were also responsible for a broad array of social welfare functions for their employees, their families, and the population of the towns and regions where they were located. Profitability and efficiency, however, were generally not the most prominent priorities for Soviet enterprise managers. Thus, almost no Soviet employees or managers had firsthand experience with decisionmaking in the conditions of a market economy.[8]

Economic Depression and Social Decay in Russia

Russia's economy sank into deep depression by the mid-1990s, was hit further by the financial crash of 1998, and then began to recover in 1999–2000. Russia's economic decline was far more severe than the Great Depression which nearly paralysed world capitalism following 1929. It is about half as severe as the catastrophic drop borne out of the consequence of the First World War, the fall of Tsarism, and the Russian Civil War. Following the economic reforms of the early 1990s, Russia suffered from a sharp increase in the rates of poverty and inequality. Estimates by the World Bank based on both macroeconomic data and surveys of household incomes and expenditures indicate that whereas 1.5 per cent of the population was living in poverty (defined as income below the equivalent of $25 per month) in the late Soviet era, by mid-1993 between 39 per cent and 49 per cent of the population was living in poverty. Per capita incomes fell by another 15 per cent by 1998, according to government figures.[9]

Public health indicators show a dramatic corresponding decline. In 1999, total population fell by about three-quarters of a million people. Meanwhile life expectancy dropped for men from sixty-four years in 1990 to fifty-seven years by 1994, while women's dropped from seventy-four to about seventy-one. Both health factors and sharp increase in deaths of mostly young people from unnatural causes (such as murders, suicides and accidents caused by increased disregard for safety) have significantly contributed to this trend. As of 2004, life expectancy is higher than at the nadir of the crisis in 1994, yet it still remains below the 1990 level.

Alcohol-related deaths skyrocketed 60 per cent in the 1990s. Deaths from infectious and parasitic diseases shot up 100 per cent, mainly because medicines were no longer affordable to the poor. There are now roughly one and half times as many deaths as births per year in Russia. While the supply shortages of consumer goods characteristic of the 1980s went away, this was not only related to the opening of Russia's market to imports in the early 1990s but also to the impoverishment of the Russian people in the 1990s. Russians on fixed incomes (the vast majority of the workforce) saw their purchasing power drastically reduced, so while the stores might have been well stocked in the Yeltsin era, workers could now afford to buy little, if anything. By 2004 the average income has risen to more than $100 per month, emblematic of the mild recovery in recent years thanks to a large extent to high oil prices. But the growing income is not being evenly distributed. The social inequality has risen sharply during the 1990s with the Gini coefficient, for example, reaching 40 per cent.[10] Russia's income disparities are now nearly as large as in Argentina and Brazil, which have long been among the world leaders in inequality, and the regional disparities in the level of poverty are still growing sharper.

Backlash against Reforms in Russia

Structural reforms lowered the standard of living for most groups of the population. Thus, reform created powerful political opposition. Democratisation opened the political channels for venting these frustrations, thus translating into votes for anti-reform candidates, especially those of the Communist Party of the Russian Federation and its allies in the parliament. Russian voters, able to vote for opposition parties in the 1990s, often rejected economic reforms and yearned for the stability and personal security of the Soviet era. These were the groups that had enjoyed the benefits of Soviet-era state-controlled wages and prices, high state spending to subsidise priority sectors of the economy, protection from competition with foreign industries, and welfare entitlement programmes. During the Yeltsin years in the 1990s, these groups were well organised, voicing their opposition to reform through strong trade unions, associations of directors of state-owned firms, and political parties in the popularly elected parliament whose primary constituencies were among those vulnerable to reform. A constant theme of Russian history in the 1990s was the conflict between economic reformers and those hostile to new capitalism.

Reform by Decree

On January 2, 1992, Yeltsin—acting as his own prime minister—enacted the most wrenching components of economic reform by decree, thereby circumventing the Supreme Soviet and Congress of People's Deputies, which had been elected in June 1991, before the dissolution of the USSR. While this spared Yeltsin from the prospects of parliamentary bargaining and wrangling, it has also destroyed the hopes for any meaningful discussion of the right course of action for the country. In retrospect, despite the great price paid by Russian people for these authoritative decisions, they did not help the country in the transition to market economy. However, radical reform still faced some critical political barriers. The Soviet-era Central Bank was still subordinate to the conservative Supreme Soviet as opposed to the presidency. During the height of hyperinflation in 1992–1993, the Central Bank actually tried to derail reforms by actively printing money during a period of inflation. After all, the Russian government was short of revenue and was forced to print money to finance its debt. As a result, inflation exploded into hyperinflation, and the Russian economy continued in a serious slump.

Clashes of Power, 1993-96 (The 1993 Constitutional Crisis)

The struggle for the center of power in post-Soviet Russia and for the nature of the economic reforms culminated in political crisis and bloodshed in the fall of 1993. Yeltsin, who represented a course of radical privatisation, was opposed by the parliament. Confronted with opposition to the presidential power of decree and threatened with impeachment, Yeltsin "dissolved" the parliament on September 21, in contravention of the existing constitution, and ordered new elections and a referendum on a new constitution. The parliament then declared Yeltsin deposed and appointed Aleksandr Rutskoy acting president on September 22. Tensions built quickly, and matters came to a head after street riots on 2 and 3 October. On October 4, Yeltsin ordered Special Forces and elite army units to storm the parliament building, the "White House"[11] as it is called. With tanks thrown against the small-arms fire of the parliamentary defenders, the outcome was not in doubt. Rutskoy, Ruslan Khasbulatov, and the other parliamentary supporters surrendered and were immediately arrested and jailed. The official count was 187 dead, 437 wounded (with several men killed and wounded on the presidential side.

Thus the transitional period in post-Soviet Russian politics came to an end. A new constitution was approved by referendum in December 1993. Russia was given a strongly presidential system. Radical privatisation went ahead. Although the old parliamentary leaders were released without trial on February 26, 1994, they would not play an open role in politics thereafter. Though, its clashes with the executive would eventually resume, the remodeled Russian parliament had greatly circumscribed powers.

First Chechen War

In 1994, Yeltsin ordered 40,000 troops to prevent the separation of the southern oil-producing region of Chechnya from Russia. Living 1,000 miles south of Moscow, the predominantly Muslim Chechens for centuries had gloried in defying the Russians. Dzhokhar Dudayev, the Republic of Chechnya's nationalist president, was driven to take his Republic out of the Russian Federation, and had declared Chechnya's independence in 1991. Russia was quickly submerged in a quagmire like that of the U.S. in the Vietnam War. When the Russians attacked the Chechen capital of Grozny during the first weeks of January 1995, about 25,000 civilians died under week-long air raids and artillery fire in the sealed-off city. Massive use of artillery and air strikes remained the dominating strategy throughout the Russian campaign. Even so, Chechen insurgents seized thousands of Russian hostages, while inflicting humiliating losses on Russia's demoralised and ill-equipped troops. Russian troops had not secured the Chechen capital of Grozny by year's end.

The Russians finally managed to gain control of Grozny in February 1995 after heavy fighting. In August 1996 Yeltsin agreed to a ceasefire with Chechen leaders, and a Peace Treaty was formally signed in May 1997.[12] However, the conflict resumed in 1999, thus rendering the 1997 peace accord meaningless Chechen rebels continue to resist the Russian presence to this day.

The "Loans for Shares" Scheme and the Rise of the "Oligarchs"

The new capitalist opportunities presented by the opening of the Russian economy in the late 1980s and early 1990s affected many people's interests. As the Soviet system was being dismantled, well-placed bosses and technocrats in the Communist Party, the KGB, and the Komsomol (Soviet Youth League) were cashing in on their Soviet-era power and privileges. Some quietly liquidated the assets of their organisation and secreted the proceeds in overseas accounts and investments.[13] Others created banks and business in Russia, taking advantage of their insider positions to win exclusive government contracts and licenses and to acquire financial credits and supplies at artificially low, state-subsidised prices in order to transact business at high, market-value prices. Great fortunes were made almost overnight.

At the same time, a few young people, without much social status, but with lots of entrepreneurial spirit, saw opportunity in the economic and legal confusion of the transition. Between 1987 and 1992, trading of natural resources and foreign currencies, as well as imports of highly demanded consumer goods and then domestic production of their rudimentary substitutes, rapidly enabled these pioneering entrepreneurs to turn accumulate considerable wealth. In turn, the emerging cash-based, highly opaque markets provided a breeding ground for a large number of racket gangs.

By the mid-nineties, the best-connected former nomenklatura leaders accumulated considerable financial resources, while on the other hand the most successful entrepreneurs became acquainted with government officials and public politicians. The privatisation of state enterprises was a unique opportunity, since it gave many of those who had gained wealth in the early 1990s a chance to convert it into shares of privatised enterprises. The Yeltsin government hoped to use privatisation to spread ownership of shares in former state enterprises as widely as possible to create political support for his government and his reforms. The government used a system of free vouchers as a way to give mass privatisation a jump-start. But it also allowed people to purchase shares of stock in privatised enterprises with cash. Even though initially each citizen received a voucher of equal face value, within months most of them converged in the hands of intermediaries who were ready to buy them for cash right away.

As the government ended the voucher privatisation phase and launched cash privatisation, it devised a programme that it thought would simultaneously speed up privatisation and yield the government a much-needed infusion of cash for its operating needs. Under the scheme, which quickly became known in the West as "loans for shares",[14] the Yeltsin regime auctioned off substantial packages of stock shares in some of its most desirable enterprises, such as energy, telecommunications and metallurgical firms, as collatoral for bank loans.

In exchange for the loans, the state handed over assets worth many times as much. Under the terms of the deals, if the Yeltsin government did not repay the loans by September 1996, the lender acquired title to the stock and could then resell it or take an equity position in the enterprise. The first auctions were held in the fall of 1995. The auctions themselves were usually held in such a way so to limit the number of banks bidding for shares and thus to keep the auction prices extremely low. By summer 1996, major packages of shares in some of Russia's largest firms had been transferred to a small number of major banks, thus allowing a handful of powerful banks to acquire substantial ownership shares over major firms at shockingly low prices. These deals were effectively giveaways of valuable state assets to a few powerful, well-connected and wealthy financial groups.

The concentration of immense financial and industrial power, which loans for shares had assisted, extended to the mass media. One of the most prominent of the financial barons, Boris

Berezovsky, who controlled major stakes in several banks and companies, exerted an extensive influence over state television programming for a while. Berezovsky and other ultra-wealthy, well-connected tycoons who controlled these great empires of finance, industry, energy, telecommunications and media became known as the "Russian oligarchs".[14] Along with Berezovsky, Mikhail Khodorkovsky, Roman Abramovich, Vladimir Potanin, Vladimir Bogdanov, Rem Viakhirev, Vagit Alekperov, Viktor Chernomyrdin, Victor Vekselberg, and Mikhail Friedman emerged as Russia's most powerful and prominent oligarchs. A tiny clique who used their connections built up during the last days of the Soviet years to appropriate Russia's vast resources during the rampant privatisations of the Yeltsin years, the oligarchs emerged as the most hated men in the nation. The Western world generally advocated a quick dismantling of the Soviet planned economy to make way for "free-market reforms," but later expressed disappointment over the newfound power and corruption of the "oligarchs."[15]

The 1996 Presidential Election: Campaigns

Early in the campaign it had been thought that Yeltsin, who was in uncertain health (after recuperating from a series of heart attacks) and whose behaviour was sometimes erratic, had little chance for reelection. When campaigning opened at the beginning of 1996, Yeltsin's popularity was close to zero. Meanwhile, the opposition Communist Party of the Russian Federation had already gained ground in parliamentary voting on December 17, 1995, and its candidate, Gennady Zyuganov, had a strong grassroots organisation, especially in the rural areas and small towns, and appealed effectively to memories of the old days of Soviet prestige on the international stage and the socialist domestic order. Panic struck the Yeltsin team when opinion polls suggested that the ailing president could not win; members of his entourage urged him to cancel presidential elections and effectively rule as dictator from then on. Instead, Yeltsin changed his campaign team, assigning a key role to his daughter, Tatyana Dyachenko, and appointing Anatoly Chubais campaign manager. Chubais, who was not just Yeltsin's campaign manager but also the architect of Russia's privatisation programme, set out to use his control of the privatisation programme as the key instrument of Yeltsin's reelection campaign.[16]

The president's inner circle assumed that it had only a short time in which to act on privatisation; it therefore needed to take steps that would have a large and immediate impact, making the reversal of reform prohibitively costly for their opponents. Chubais's solution was to co-opt potentially powerful interests, including enterprise directors and regional officials, in order to ensure Yeltsin's reelection. The position of the enterprise directors to the programme was essential to maintaining economic and social stability in the country. The managers represented one of the most powerful collective interests in the country; it was the enterprise managers who could ensure that labour did not erupt in a massive wave of strikes. The government, therefore, did not strenuously resist the tendency for voucher privatisation to turn into "insider privatisation,"[17] as it was termed, in which senior enterprise officials acquired the largest proportion of shares in privatised firms. Thus, Chubais allowed well-connected employees to acquire majority stakes in the enterprises. This proved to be the most widely used form of privatisation in Russia. Three-quarters of privatised enterprises opted for this method, most often using vouchers. Real control thus wound up in the hands of the managers.

Support from the oligarchs was also crucial to Yeltsin's reelection campaign. The "loans for shares" giveaway took place in the run-up to the 1996 presidential election—at a point when it had appeared that Zyuganov might defeat Yeltsin. Yeltsin and his entourage gave the oligarchs an opportunity to scoop up some of Russia's most desirable assets in return for their help in his reelection effort. The oligarchs, in turn, reciprocated the favour.[18]

In the spring of 1996, with Yeltsin's popularity at a low ebb, Chubais and Yeltsin recruited a team of six leading Russian financiers and media barons (all oligarchs) who bankrolled the Yeltsin campaign with $3 million and guaranteed coverage on television and in leading newspapers directly serving the president's campaign strategy. The media painted a picture of a fateful choice for Russia, between Yeltsin and a "return to totalitarianism."[19] The oligarchs even played up the threat of civil war if a Communist were elected president.

In the outlying regions of the country, the Yeltsin campaign relied on its ties to other allies—the patron-client ties of the local governors, most of whom had been appointed by the president. The Zyuganov campaign had a strong grass-roots organisation, but it was simply no match to the financial resources and access to patronage that the Yeltsin campaign could marshal. Yeltsin campaigned energetically, dispelling concerns about his health, exploiting all the advantages of incumbency to maintain a high media profile. To assuage voters' discontent, he made the claim that he would abandon some unpopular economic reforms and boost welfare spending, end the war in Chechnya, pay wage and pension arrears, and abolish the military draft programme (he did not live up to his promises after the election, except for ending the Chechen war, which was halted for three years). Yeltsin's campaign also got a boost from the announcement of a $10 billion loan to the Russian government from the International Monetary Fund.[20]

Grigory Yavlinsky was the liberal alternative to Yeltsin and Zyuganov. He appealed to a well-educated middle class that saw Yeltsin as a drunken scoundrel and Zyuganov as a Soviet-era throwback. Seeing Yavlinsky as a threat, Yeltsin's inner circle of supporters worked to bifurcate political discourse, thus excluding a middle ground—and convince voters that only Yeltsin could defeat the Communist 'menace'. The election became a two-man race, and Zyuganov, who lacked Yeltsin's resources and financial backing, watched haplessly as his strong initial lead was whittled away.

Elections

Voter turnout in the first round of the polling on June 16 was 69.8 per cent. According to returns announced on June 17, Yeltsin won 35 per cent of the vote; Zyuganov won 32 per cent; Aleksandr Lebed, a populist ex-general, a surprisingly high 14.5 per cent; liberal candidate Grigory Yavlinsky 7.4 per cent; far-right nationalist Vladimir Zhirinovsky 5.8 per cent; and former Soviet president Mikhail Gorbachev 0.5 per cent.[21] With no candidate securing an absolute majority, Yeltsin and Zyuganov went into a second round of voting. In the meantime, Yeltsin co-opted a large segment of the electorate by appointing Lebed to the posts of National Security Adviser and Secretary of the Security Council.

In the end, Yeltsin's election tactics paid off. In the run-off on July 3, with a turnout of 68.9 per cent, Yeltsin won 53.8 per cent of the vote and Zyuganov 40.3 per cent, with the rest (5.9 per cent) voting "against all".[22] Moscow and St. Petersburg (formerly Leningrad) together provided over half of the incumbent president's support, but he also did well in large cities in the Urals and in the north and northeast. Yeltsin lost to Zyuganov in Russia's southern industrial heartland. The southern stretch of the country became known as the "red belt", underscoring the resilience of the Communist Party in elections since the breakup of the Soviet Union.[23]

Although, Yeltsin promised that he would abandon his unpopular neoliberal austerity policies and increase public spending to help those suffering from the pain of capitalist reforms, within a month of his election, Yeltsin issued a decree canceling almost all of these promises. Right after the election, Yeltsin's physical health and mental stability were increasingly precarious. Many of Yeltsin's executive functions thus devolved upon a group of advisers (most of whom had close links with the oligarchs).

Crises of 1998

The global recession of 1998, which started with the Asian financial crisis in July 1997, exacerbated Russia's economic crisis. Given the ensuing decline in world commodity prices, countries heavily dependent on the export of raw materials such as oil were among those most severely hit. (Oil, natural gas, metals, and timber account for more than 80 per cent of Russian exports, leaving the country vulnerable to swings in world prices.) Oil is also a major source of government tax revenue.[24] The sharp decline in the price of oil had severe consequences for Russia.

The pressures on the ruble, reflecting the weakness of the economy, resulted in a disastrous fall in the value of the currency. Massive tax evasion also continued, and the government found itself unable to service the massive loans it had received or even to pay its employees. The government stopped making timely payment of wages, pensions and debts to suppliers; and when workers were paid, it was often with bartered goods rather than rubles. Coal miners were hard hit, and for several weeks in the summer they blocked sections of the Trans-Siberian railroad, effectively cutting the country in two. As time wore on, they added calls for the resignation of Yeltsin and his government to their wage demands.[25]

A political crisis came to a head in March when Yeltsin suddenly dismissed Prime Minister Viktor Chernomyrdin and his entire cabinet on March 23. Yeltsin named a virtually unknown technocrat, Energy Minister Sergei Kiriyenko, aged 35, as acting prime minister. Russian observers expressed doubts about Kiriyenko's youth and inexperience. The Duma rejected his nomination twice. Only after a month-long standoff, during which Yeltsin threatened to dissolve the legislature, did the Duma confirm Kiriyenko on a third vote on April 24. Kiriyenko appointed a new cabinet strongly committed to stemming the fall in value of Russia's currency. The oligarchs strongly supported Kiriyenko's efforts to maintain the exchange rate. A high exchange rate meant that they needed fewer rubles to buy imported goods, especially luxury items.[26]

In an effort to prop up the currency and stem the flight of capital, Kiriyenko hiked interest rates to 150 per cent in order to attract buyers for government bonds. But concerns about the financial crisis in Asia and the slump in world oil prices were already prompting investors to withdraw from Russia. By mid-1998, it was clear Russia would need help from IMF to maintain its exchange rate. The Russian crisis caused alarm in the West. Pouring more money into the Russian economy would not be a long-term solution, but the US in particular feared that Yeltsin's government would not survive a looming financial crisis without IMF help. US President Bill Clinton's treasury secretary, Robert Rubin, also feared that a Russian collapse could create a panic on world money markets (and it indeed did help bring down one major U.S. fund). The IMF approved a $22.6 billion emergency loan on July 13.[27]

Despite the bailout, Russia's monthly interest payments still well exceeded its monthly tax revenues. Realising that this situation was unsustainable, investors continued to flee Russia despite the IMF bailout. Weeks later the financial crisis resumed as and the value of the ruble resumed its fall, and the government fell into a self perpetuating trap. To pay off the interest on the loans it had taken, it needed to raise still more cash, which it did through foreign borrowing. As lenders became increasingly certain that the government could not make good on its obligations, they demanded ever-higher interest rates, deepening the trap. Ultimately the bubble burst.

On August 17, 1997 Kiriyenko's government and the central bank were forced to suspend payment on Russia's foreign debt for 90 days, restructure the nation's entire debt, and devalue the ruble. The ruble went into free fall as Russians sought frantically to buy dollars. Western creditors lost heavily, and a large part of Russia's fledgling banking sector was destroyed, since many banks had substantial dollar borrowings. Foreign investment rushed out of the country, and financial crisis triggered an unprecedented flight of capital from Russia.[28]

Political Fallout

The financial collapse produced a political crisis, as Yeltsin, with his domestic support evaporating, had to contend with an emboldened opposition in the parliament. A week later, on August 23, Yeltsin fired Kiryenko and declared his intention of returning Chernomyrdin to office as the country slipped deeper into economic turmoil. Powerful business interests, fearing another round of reforms that might cause leading concerns to fail, welcomed Kiriyenko's fall, as did the Communists. Yeltsin, who began to lose his hold as his health deteriorated, wanted Chernomyrdin back, but the legislature refused to give its approval. After the Duma rejected Chernomyrdin's candidacy twice, Yeltsin's power clearly on the decline, backed down. Instead, he nominated Foreign Minister Yevgeny Primakov, who on September 11 was overwhelmingly approved by the Duma. Primakov's appointment restored political stability because he was seen as a compromise candidate able to heal the rifts between Russia's quarrelling interest groups. There was popular enthusiasm for Primakov as well. Primakov promised to make the payment of wage and pension arrears his government's first priority, and invited members of the leading parliamentary factions into his Cabinet.[29]

Communists and trade unionists staged a nationwide strike on October 7, and called on President Yeltsin to resign. On

October 9, Russia, which was also suffering from a bad harvest, appealed for international humanitarian aid, including food.

Recovery

Russia bounced back from the August 1998 financial crash with surprising speed. Much of the reason for the recovery is that world oil prices rapidly rose during 1999-2000 (just as falling energy prices on the world market helped to deepen Russia's financial troubles), so that Russia ran a large trade surplus in 1999 and 2000. Another reason is that domestic industries such as food processing have benefited from the devaluation, which caused a steep increase in the prices of imported goods.[30] Also, since Russia's economy was operating to such a large extent on barter and other non-monetary instruments of exchange, the financial collapse had far less of an impact on many producers than it would had the economy been dependent on a banking system. Finally, the economy has been helped by an infusion of cash; as enterprises were able to pay off arrears in back wages and taxes, it in turn allowed consumer demand for the goods and services of Russian industry to rise. For the first time in many years, unemployment in 2000 fell as enterprises added workers. Nevertheless, the political and social equilibrium of the country remains tenuous to this day, and power remains a highly personalised commodity. The economy remains vulnerable to downturn if, for instance, world oil prices fall at a dramatic pace.[31]

Succession Crisis, 1999-2000

Yevgeny Primakov did not remain in his post long. Yeltsin grew suspicious that Primakov was gaining in strength and popularity so dismissed him in May 1999, after only eight months in office.[32] Yeltsin then named Sergei Stepashin, who had formerly been head of the FSB (the successor agency to the KGB) and later been Interior Minister, to replace him. The Duma confirmed his appointment on the first ballot by a wide margin. Stephashin's tenure was even shorter than Primakov's. In August 1999, Yeltsin once again abruptly dismissed the government and named Vladimir Putin as his candidate to head the new government. Like Stephashin, Putin had a background in the secret police, having made his career in the foreign intelligence service. Yeltsin went so far as to declare that he saw Putin as his successor as President. The Duma narrowly voted to confirm Putin.

When appointed, Putin was a relatively unknown politician, but he quickly established himself both in public opinion and in Yeltsin's estimation as a trusted head of government, largely due to the Second Chechen War. Just days after Yeltsin named Putin as a candidate for prime minister, Chechen forces engaged the Russian army in Dagestan, a Russian autonomy near Chechnya. In the next month, several hundred people died in apartment building bombings in Moscow and other cities, bombings Russian authorities attributed to Chechen rebels. In response, the Russian army entered Chechnya in late September 1999, starting the Second Chechen War. The Russian public at the time, angry over the terrorist bombings, widely supported the war. The support translated into growing popularity for Putin, who had taken decisive action in Chechnya.

After the success of political forces close to Putin in the December 1999 parliamentary elections, Yeltsin evidentially felt confident enough in Putin that he resigned from the Presidency on December 31, six months before his term was due to expire. This made Putin acting President and gave Putin ample opportunity to position himself as frontrunner for the Russian Presidential election held on March 26, 2000, which he won. The Chechen War figured prominently in the campaign. In February 2000, Russian troops entered Grozny, the Chechen capital, and a week before the election, Putin flew to Chechnya on a fighter jet, claiming victory.[33]

The Putin Administration, 2000-Present

In August 2000, the Russian submarine K-141 Kursk suffered an explosion, causing the submarine to sink in the shallow area of the Barents Sea. Russia organised a vigorous but hectic attempt to save the crew, and the entire futile effort was surrounded by unexplained secrecy. This, as well as the slow initial reaction to the event and especially to the offers of foreign aid in saving the crew, brought much criticism on the government and personally on President Putin.

On October 23, 2002, Chechen rebels took over a Moscow theater. Over 700 people inside were taken hostage in what has been called the Moscow theater hostage crisis.[34] The rebels demanded the immediate withdrawal of Russian forces from Chechnya and threatened to blow up the building if authorities attempted to enter. Three days later, Russian commandos stormed the building after the hostages had been subdued with a sleeping gas, shooting the unconscious militants. The gas, which Russian officials refused to identify to doctors treating the hostages, was implicated as the cause of death for over 115 hostages. In the aftermath of the theater siege, Putin began renewed efforts to eliminate the Chechen insurrection. The government cancelled scheduled troop withdrawals, surrounded Chechen refugee camps with soldiers, and increased the frequency of assaults on rebel positions.

The Chechens responded in kind, stepping up guerrilla operations and rocket attacks on federal helicopters. Several high-profile attacks have taken place. In May 2004, Chechen rebels assassinated Akhmad Kadyrov, the pro-Russia Chechen leader who became the president of Chechnya eight months earlier after an election conducted by Russian authorities. On August 24, 2004, two Russian aircraft were bombed. This was followed by the Beslan school hostage crisis in which Chechen rebels took 1,300 hostages. The initially high public support for the war in Chechnya has declined. Only 19 per cent of Russians supported continuing military action in September 2006, according to a Levada-Center poll.[35]

Putin has confronted several very influential oligarchs (Vladimir Gusinsky, Boris Berezovsky and Mikhail Khodorkovsky, in particular) who attained large stakes of state assets, allegedly through illegal schemes, during the privatisation process. Gusinsky and Berezovsky have been forced to leave Russia and give up parts of their assets. Khodorkovsky is jailed in Russia and has lost his YUKOS company, formerly the largest oil producer in Russia. Putin's stand against oligarchs is generally popular with the Russian people, even though the jailing of Khodorkovsky is mainly seen as part of a takeover operation by government officials, according to another Levada-Centre poll.

These confrontations have also lead to Putin establishing control over Russian media outlets previously owned by the oligarchs. In 2001 and 2002, TV channels NTV (previously owned by Gusinsky), TV6 and TVS (owned by Berezovsky) were all taken over by media groups loyal to Putin. Similar takeovers have also occurred with print media.

Putin's administration exercises a significant control over the content in Russian media. Most editors and managers are willing to pull an article or to fire a journalist upon an informal request from the presidential administration. While many of Yeltsin-era problems (such as war in Chechnya and strikes over unpaid wages) still exist, journalists are now asked to ignore or downplay them, producing a positive picture of Russia.[36]

Putin's popularity, which stems from his reputation as a strong leader, stands in contrast to the unpopularity of his predecessor, but it hinges on a continuation of economic recovery. Putin came into office at an ideal time: after the devaluation of the ruble in 1998, which boosted demand for domestic goods, and while world oil prices were rising. Indeed, during the seven years of his presidency, real GDP grew on average 6.7 per cent a year, average income increased 11 per cent annually in real terms, and a consistently positive balance of the federal budget enabled the government to cut 70 per cent of the external debt (according to the Institute for Complex Strategic Studies). Thus, many credit him with the recovery, but his ability to withstand a sudden economic downturn has been untested. Putin won the Russian presidential election in 2004 without any significant competition.[37]

Some researchers assert that most Russians today have come to regret the collapse of the Soviet Union in 1991. On repeated occasions, even Vladimir Putin—Boris Yeltsin's handpicked successor — stated that the fall of Soviet rule had led to few gains and many problems for most Russian citizens. In a campaign speech in February 2004, for example, Putin called the dismantlement of the Soviet Union a "national tragedy on an enormous scale," from which "only the elites and nationalists of the republics gained."[38] He added, "I think that ordinary citizens of the former Soviet Union and the post-Soviet space gained nothing from this. On the contrary, people have faced a huge number of problems."[39]

Putin's international prestige suffered a major blow in the West during the disputed 2004 Ukrainian presidential election.

Putin had twice visited Ukraine before the election to show his support for the pro-Russian Viktor Yanukovych against opposition leader Viktor Yushchenko, a pro-Western liberal economist. He also congratulated Yanukovych on his victory before election results were even made official and made statements opposing the rerun of the disputed second round of elections, won by Yanukovych, amid allegations of large-scale voting fraud. The second round was ultimately rerun; Yushchenko won the round and was eventually declared the winner on January 10, 2005. In the West, the reaction to Russia's handling of, or perhaps interference in, the Ukrainian election evoked echoes of the cold war, but relations with the US have remained stable.

In 2005, the Russian government replaced the broad in-kind Soviet-era benefits, such as free transportation and subsidies for heating and other utilities for socially vulnerable groups by cash payments. The reform, known as monetisation,[40] has been unpopular and caused a wave of demonstrations in various Russian cities, with thousands of retirees protesting against the loss of their benefits. This was the first time such wave of protests took place during the Putin administration. The reform has hurt the popularity of the Russian government, but Putin personally is still popular, with a 77 per cent approval rating.

Russia's Relationship with the West

In the early period after Russia became independent, Russian foreign policy repudiated Marxism-Leninism as a recognised guide to action, emphasizing cooperation with the West in solving regional and global problems, and soliciting economic and humanitarian aid from the West in support of internal economic reforms. However, although Russia's leaders now described the West as its natural ally, they grappled with defining new relations with the East European states, the new states formed upon the disintegration of Yugoslavia and Western Europe. Russia opposed the expansion of NATO into the former Soviet bloc nations of the Czech Republic, Poland, and Hungary in 1997 and, particularly, the second NATO expansion into Baltic states in 2004. In 1999, Russia opposed the NATO bombing of Yugoslavia for more than two months, but later joined NATO peacekeeping forces in the Balkans in June 1999.

Relations with the West have also been stained by Russia's relationship with Belarus. Belarusian President Alexander Lukashenko, an authoritarian Soviet-style leader, has shown much interest in aligning his country with Russia, and no interest in deepening ties with the ever-expanding NATO or implementing Western-backed neoliberal economic reforms. A union agreement between Russia and Belarus was formed on April 2, 1996. The agreement was tightened, becoming the Union of Russia and Belarus on April 3, 1997. Further strengthening of the union occurred on December 25, 1998, and in 1999. Under Putin, Russia has sought to strengthen ties with the People's Republic of China by signing the Treaty of Good-Neighbourliness and Friendly Cooperation as well building the Trans-Siberian oil pipeline geared toward Chinese growing energy needs. He also made a number of appearances in the media with President of the United States George W. Bush in which the two described each other as "friends"– at least before the Iraq War.[41]

Change and Continuity in Post-Soviet Russian Culture

Contemporary Russian culture is rooted in the legacies of the Soviet regime and the thousand-year heritage of the Russian state. The Soviet Union, itself the heir of a Tsarist state that had gained control of the major part of the Eurasian landmass over hundreds of years, seemed profoundly resistant to change just shortly before its collapse. Beneath the official propaganda, however, interest in both pre-Soviet traditions and the ways of the West grew during the so-called "period of stagnation".[42] Russia inherited from the Soviet Union a diverse cultural heritage. Throughout the Soviet Union, intellectuals, artists, and teachers preserved over a hundred different cultural legacies and national languages. Even in the most repressive years of Stalinism, private life survived—lasting to this day—formed through strong family and friendship links. So too did a legacy of the Tsarist era through the great classic works of pre-revolutionary literature and art that generations of Soviet schoolchildren and university students were taught to respect and study.

The imperative of providing the Soviet regime with a powerful scientific and technological capacity also required the regime to accept a certain level of openness and outside influences: scientific and cultural exchanges of people and ideas kept open channels through which the diverse influences of the outside world and especially the West filtered in the Soviet Union. As the Communist regime's machinery for shaping public values and reinforcing CPSU-rule (youth groups, the mass media, and Party-run workplace education) grew increasingly ossified and ineffectual after Stalin's death, these internal and external cultural influences assumed an ever-greater importance in shaping Soviet politics, culture and public opinion.

As the old regime's system for shaping public values and beliefs was breaking down in the late 1980s and 1990s, non-communist ideologies such as liberal democracy, religious faith, and ethnic nationalism saw a revival. At the moment of collapse in 1991, a significant proportion of the population, likely the absolute majority, looked hopefully to the future. However, as the Utopian vision of a prosperous and peaceful democracy gave place to the troubled and insecure reality, many became nostalgic for the days of the old Soviet superpower. The word best applied to post-Soviet Russian culture is *eclectic*. While coming to grips with, and in no way rejecting fully, the Soviet inheritance, Russians reached out to identify with their own pre-Soviet past and embraced, some would say indiscriminately, tendencies from the West.

A very public debate has been waged about the nation's history. Revisionism has extended not merely to reappraisals of attitude, but to the chronological timeline itself (for example, the theories of Anatoly Fomenko). Nicholas the Bloody has become St. Nicholas the Martyr in various circles; Lenin would be buried by half the population; toponymy has achieved a balance between the Soviet and the Imperial past. But the present has had the greatest effect. Economic and political upheaval quickly made some of the formerly most respected or stable professions among the least desirable in material terms. Teachers worked for months without pay in some cases. Scientific workers lived on the poverty line or were thrown out of work when their research institutes were closed. The members of the artistic and cultural elites also had to learn to subsist with greatly diminished levels of support from the state. Some wilted, some emigrated, and some adapted.

The Russian Orthodox Church has grown rapidly since 1991, as churches and monasteries have reopened and been restored, often by the work of their congregation. At the same time, Slavic neo-pagans have made their appearance. So too have foreign sects and other religions. Their proselytising has been controversial, however, and has had to face roadblocks from the state and from some of the citizens. Still, though the holidays of Easter and Christmas have been reinstated (according to the Julian calendar), church attendance has grown substantially compared to Soviet era, and heretofore virtually non-existent rituals such as church weddings have become common, most Russians have remained, if not confessed atheists, quite unobservant.

The younger generation, especially, has embraced Western music and other types of pop culture. That and the growth of advertising has affected the Russian language, as many English words and constructions have become wildly fashionable. Drug abuse, which was kept tightly under wraps during the Soviet era, has come into the open with disastrous consequences. Today in Russia there are more than three million drug addicts. Heroin appears to be the drug of choice. Fueled by sharing needles by drug addicts, the AIDS epidemic is rampant - the number of HIV-positive people increased from less than 100 in 1989 to more than one million in 2005.

While it took the publishing industry some time to switch from massive state orders to the consumer market, Russia remains a highly literate nation with considerable interest in literature. Crime fiction, romance novels, alternative history, and historical novels are popular and commercially successful. Conversely, poetry has declined. Spectator sports continued as a welcome diversion. Overwhelming successes at the Olympics and the great national ice hockey teams have become things of the past. Russian tennis players, on the other hand, have achieved highly profiled success.

The attitude to the rest of the world has seen great perturbations. If in 1991 overall consensus toward the West was favorable indeed, it was quickly dimmed by the economic disruptions induced by the indiscriminate and corrupt privatisations. Many Russians perceived a continued distrust or even hostility from Europe and the United States. A sense of

Russian political isolation was encouraged by overt political actions, especially NATO's 1999 bombing of Serbia over Kosovo.

Thus a split became all too apparent. Many Russians, especially of the older generation, came to see the so-called "era of stagnation" under Brezhnev as a kind of stable golden age.[43] A few, more visible than strong in numbers, placed their aspirations on Stalin. Letters in newspapers and the occasional leading article made it clear that by 2005, at a moment of relative stability, many felt like immigrants in their own country. Russians who prospered or survived under the changed conditions often mocked the nostalgia. In the end, however, reither age nor material conditions fully determined the outlook. The strongest continuation in Russian outlook from the later Soviet period is that most citizens do not in any sense identify their culture with their government, or (to a somewhat lesser extent) with political ideology. Among the most controversial breaks with the past, if the tendency does not prove temporary, may be a post-imperial national awareness that places greater emphasis on ethnic belonging. Personal hostility from ethnic Russians to the so-called "national minorities" in widespread, assisted by demographics and based on perception of internal and international politics, appears to be considerably stronger than in the Soviet period. Overall, the official line today is a neutral acknowledgement of all phases of Russian history and culture. Underneath the circles of power, Russians are divided, as in ages past, between the "Westernisers" and the "Slavophiles" or "Eurasians", though it is too early either to speak of these tendencies as formal movements or to predict which one will prevail. At present, a kind of dynamic equilibrium appears to have been achieved after the chaos of the first post-Soviet years, but its permanence remains to be seen.

References

1. Anders Aslund, "How small is the Soviet National Income?" in Henry S. Rowen and Charles Wolf, Jr., eds., *The Impoverished Superpower: Perestroika and the Soviet Military Burden*, San Francisco: Institute for Contemporary Studies, 1990, p. 49.
2. Ibid., p.49.

3. For example, see the discussion of this point in Anders Åslund, *How Russia Became a Market Economy*, Washington D.C.: Brookings Institution, 1995, p.154.
4. Ibid., p.155.
5. See, e.g., "State Department Background Notes on Russia in 1991-1995" excerpted from *The Soviet Union— A Country Study*, Raymond E. Zickel, ed. (Washington, D. C.: Federal Research Division of the Library of Congress, 1989). This can be read online at http://unx1.shsu.edu/ ~his_ncp/Soviet2.html.
6. For example, see Sheila M. Puffer, ed., *The Russian Management Revolution: Preparing Managers for the Market Economy*, Armonk, NY: M.E. Sharpe, 1992.
7. Ibid.
8. Ibid.
9. http://lcweb2.loc.gov/cgi-bin/query/r?frd/cstdy:@field(DOCID+ru0119).
10. It is still hotly debated among Western economists, social scientists, and policymakers as to whether or not the IMF-, World Bank-, and U.S. Treasury Department-backed reform policies adopted in Russia, often called "shock therapy," were responsible for Russia's poor record of economic performance in the 1990s. A similar reform programme had been adopted in Poland in January 1990, with generally favorable results. However, Western critics of Yeltsin's reform, most notably Marshall Goldman, Stephen Cohen, and Joseph Stiglitz (who would have favored a more "gradual" transition to market capitalism), consider policies adopted in Poland ill-suited for Russia, given that the impact of communism on the Polish economy and political culture was far less indelible. http://www.imf.org/external/np /vc/2002/082602.htm
11. The poverty line in 1993 was set at the equivalent of $25 per month. The difference in estimates is due to the difference in methodology. The higher poverty rate is based on a calculation of household incomes. The lower rate is based on household consumption, since households tend not to report some portion on the monthly income.
12. Branko Milanovic, *Income, Inequality, and Poverty During the Transformation from Planned to Market Economy*, Washington DC: The World Bank, 1998, pp.186-90.
13. https://www.cia.gov/cia/publications/factbook/geos/rs.html
14. Ibid.
15. Ibid.

16. The purported suicide of Nikolai Kruchina, who managed the Communist Party's financial affairs, following the collapse of the August 1991 coup attempt, deprived future researchers of the opportunity to discover where many of the party's assets disappeared.
17. Ibid.
18. CNN, Russian presidential candidate profiles, 1906.http://edition.cnn.com/WORLD/pivotal.elections/96/russia/candidate.html.
19. Ibid.
20. CNN, Gennady Zyuganov candidate profile, 1996. http://edition.cnn.com/WORLD/9602/russia_zyuganov.
21. http://vms.cc.wmich.edu/~97levintova/Ny.html.
22. Ibid.
23. Ibid.
24. See, e.g., Pekka Sutela, "Insider Privatisation in Russia: Speculations on Systemic Changes," *Europe-Asia Studies* 46:3 (1994), pp. 420-21.
25. Ibid.
26. Daniel Treisman, "Blaming Russia First," *Foreign Affairs*, Nov/Dec. 2000. http://www.foreignaffairs.org/20001101fare viewessay946/daniel-treisman/ blaming-russia-first.html.
27. http://edition.cnn.com/WORLD/pivotal.elections/1996/russia/candidate.html.
28. Ibid.
29. http://media.washingtonpost.com/wpsrv/inatl/longterm/russiagov/stories/premier070596.htm.
30. http://www.pbs.org/newshour/bb/europe/july96/runoff_results1_7-4.html.
31. http://www.cia.gov/cia/publications/factbook/geos/rs.html.
32. http://www.pbs.org/newshour/bb/europe/july-dec98/russia_10-27.html
33. http://www.pbs.org/newshour/bb/europe/jan-june98/russia_3-23.html
34. http://www.cnn.com/WORLD/europe/9804/24/duma.vote.results/.
35. http://www.worldbank.org/html/prddr/trans/mayjune2002/pgs14-17.htm Excerpts from Globalisation and Its Discontents]. By Joseph Stiglitz. *Beyond Transition. The newsletter about reforming economies.* The World Bank Group. Volume 13, Number 3, May-June 2002.

36. http://www.pbs.org/wgbh/commandingheights/shared/minitextlo/int_robertrubin.html#6.
37. http://www.pbs.org/newshour/bb/europe/july-dec98/russia_7-13.html
38. http://www.jamestown.org/publications_details.php?volume_id=5&issue_id=293&article_id=3285
39. http://www.pbs.org/newshour/forum/september98/russia.html
40. http://education.guardian.co.uk/higher/comment/story/0%2C9828%2C932847%2C00.html
41. http://www.jamestown.org/publications_details.php?volume_id=6&&issue_id=368
42. http://jamestown.org/publicationsdetails.php?volume_id=2&&issue_id=21.
43. http://www.washtimes.com/upi-breaking/20041229-025404-5878r.htm

    http://www.theglobeandmail.com/servlet/story/RTGAM.20040212.wsovi0212/BNPrint/Front

3

Indo-Russian Economic and Trade Relations during the Post-Cold War Period (1991-2003)

Introduction

India and the former Soviet Union had close political and economic ties for over four decades before the dissolution of the USSR. The Soviet Union played a major role in the development of several basic industries in India including steel, mining, heavy engineering, power and so on. It was an important trading partner of India accounting for 12-15 per cent of India's foreign trade. Even after the disintegration, sustained close and friendly political relations built over the previous decades. There are no conflicts of interest between India and Russia, and what is equally significant is that there is commonality of views between the two countries on various international issues. Notwithstanding these positive elements in the relations between the two countries, economic ties between India and Russia are far from satisfactory. An effort has been made in this paper to highlight and analyse some of the aspects concerning trade and economic relations between the two countries.[1]

Since the early 90s, there has been a tapering down of trade between India and Russia and today it is less than US$ three billion. The trade relations between India and Russia are not living up to real potentials. Overall strategic partnership will weaken if the trade aspect of the Indio-Russian bilateral relations is not given a boost. At the governmental and political level, there is a definite desire to establish business-to-business partnerships. The Indian Government too is willing to take initiatives to carry the dialogue and iron out the differences between the two countries. The Russian side too is dealing with the technical problems it is facing. The dissolution of the Soviet Union in 1991 was the primary reason for a slowdown in trade and relations between India and Russia. However, as the Russian economy has stabilised, relations with India too have accelerated, if not in substance, at least in intent. Therefore, in the present chapter an attempt has been made to probe the economic and trade relations between India and Russia during the post-cold war period.[2]

Indo-Russian Trade and Economic Relations in the 1990's

One important point of the old Indo-Soviet friendship was a special bilateral trade and economic relationship. Although, this arrangement had many usual weaknesses like corruption, patronage transactions in low quality products, it helped many small and medium size private Indian companies to become exporters. After the disintegration of the Soviet Union, this relationship has been badly damaged. Economic transformation in Russia from a centrally planned economy to a market economy in 1992 coincided with the policies of economic liberalisation in India. These developments changed the nature and character of foreign economic relations in both the countries. Therefore, despite having solid economic and trade relations in the past, a large part of the 1990's was a period of difficult adjustments, both for Indian as well as Russian businesses. In the last few years, however, things are beginning to change.

The decade of the 1990's was a very difficult period for Russian business. It was not only that Russia was transforming its economic system, but this transformation was also taking place in a period, when Russian economy faced one crisis after another. As a result, the Russian economy was already reduced to half of what it was in 1990, when another financial and economic crisis hit the economy in August 1998. In contrast, the Indian economy in the 1990's grew fast, compared to any other time in the recent past. The average annual growth rate between 1990 and 2000 was minus 4.8 per cent for Russia and about 6 per cent for India. So, Indo-Russian economic relations also have to be looked within this context. In the last five years, the Russian economy has experienced a strong growth. Still, the Indian private sector is very slow in taking advantage from sustained Russian growth. Bilateral economic relations are surviving mainly because of defense purchases, protection to Indian exporters and some public sector investments by India.[3]

The Indo-Russian relations in the Yeltsin period can be classified into two phases. While the initial two years were difficult in shaping the bilateral relations, the later years saw gradual evolution of relations in a steady manner. The Russian foreign policy in the first phase was guided by an overarching sense of 'enlightened pragmatism' that was neither enlightened nor pragmatic, but a 'mistake' (as former Russian Foreign Minister and later Prime Minister, Yevgeny Primakov observed it).[4] As a result, the short-lived first phase had to enter the second phase wherein Russia started considering itself a 'Eurasian country' since more of its part lies in Asia than in Europe. These new developments took place because of the "shift in Russian domestic and foreign policy that became evident in the second half of 1992."[5] Thus, the Indo-Russian relations revived in the second phase. The two countries reoriented their relations keeping in view the changing realities in the changing world order. By the end of the period the bilateral relations were on a stable and positive course. The Yeltsin visit to India in 1993 was considered as a first step in that direction.

The initial years in bilateral relations aftermath of the Soviet disintegration was not only uncertain but also marked by a high degree of suspicion. In this period of transition from a socialist pattern of society to market economy, marked by turbulence in every aspect of Russia society, polity, economy and culture, the leadership gave up the traditional approach towards its old allies including India. In the post-confrontation, post-communist world, the focus was on democracy, market reforms and pluralism, for which, the leaders thought, western aid was essential. Nevertheless the sudden shift in the priority areas proved costly for the Russia-Gulf crisis, Yogoslavia crisis and cryogenic rocket controversy, etc., which provided ample proofs of Russia's weakness. It was thus on expected lines that its relations with India should get affected in 1991-92.

Besides the collapse of the Soviet Union, the forces of globalisation too affected bilateral economic relations. It can be mentioned here that both India and Russia launched the policies of liberalisation and market reforms in 1991. Both were facing, as President Yeltsin visualised, 'mostly the same problems', and for the solution of these problems the Russian leader suggested, "we are to cope with enormous economic and social tasks, and cooperation between India and Russia in this area could prove useful and important."[6] However, as the later developments, such as rupee–rouble crisis, cryogenic rocket controversy and Russia's attitude on Kashmir revealed, economic relations were not smooth between the two countries. However, within a time frame of about two years, the Russian romanticism with the West came to a halt and it turned towards the old allies.

President Boris Yeltsin's visit to India in January 1993 marked the beginning of a new phase in Indo-Russian relations. The visit ended all speculations regarding the deteriorating relations between the two countries. One major development that took place after 1993 was the increasing level of defence cooperation between India and Russia. It was not secret that Indian military establishment had been dependent on Russian spares in India were 40, 64 and 80 per cents for the army, the air force and the navy respectively. Though, starting with a disappointing note after the disintegration of the Soviet Union, the Russian cooperation in the field of defence increased gradually. For instance, the countries signed an agreement on military cooperation on 22 October 1996, during the visit of Russian Defence Minister, General Igor Rodionov to New Delhi. Indian Defence Minister, Mulayam Singh Yadav, during his visit to Moscow in October 1996, signed an agreement to extend military-to-military cooperation that would last till the year 2010. President Yeltsin, during his discussions with Yadav, repeatedly referred to his country's relations with India 'brotherly'.[7]

The uncertainty regarding the cooperation in the nuclear field was overcome gradually in the later phase of the Yeltsin period. The Russian leaders, during the visit of Indian External Affairs Minister, I.K. Gujaral, to Moscow in February 1997, reiterated that Moscow would honour its commitment to sell nuclear reactors to India. The Russian Parliament, on 14 March 1997, approved with applause the statement that each one of its factions supports the policy of cooperation with India. This was an indication of the overwhelming public support in Russia for strengthening relations with India. This also served as a reliable pointer for the forthcoming visit by the Indian Prime Minister, H.D. Deve Gowda to the Russian capital in March 1997, in which both the countries discussed the policy of nuclear cooperation. One of the major purposes of the Deve Gowda's visit was to finalise the purchase of two 1000 MW nuclear power reactors. The negotiation for the sale of reactors had started in 1988 but Russia started dillydallying after the 1992 Nuclear Suppliers Group Pact; it was bowing to the US pressure. It became doubtful if the reactors would ever be supplied. Since the proposal dated back to 1998, it could escape the provisions of the pact. To nullify the American pressure, the Russian leaders assured Deve Gowda that no third country could have any say on their bilateral relations.[8]

However, the 1990s represented one of the most difficult decades in Indo-Russian relations. Though the initial two years were almost non-starters in bilateral relations as discussed earlier, it was only with the visit of then Russian President Yeltsin that the relations gathered momentum. Though politico-strategic relations became strengthened, the post–1993 phase was not much enthusiastic from the point of view of economic cooperation. It was in the decade of the 2000s that both the countries realised the imperative of economic cooperation.

According to government sources, trade between India and Russia declined from $ 2,368 millions in 1991–92 to $ 1,569 millions in 1997-98, i.e., a drop of over 30 per cent in about seven years. Trade between the two countries declined sharply in the first half of the 1990s, which was a crisis period immediately after the Soviet break–up. This indicated the severe impact of the Soviet break-up in the India–Russia economic trade. An important aspect of bilateral trade was high fluctuations in trade over the years, which indicated lack of stability in trade relations between the two countries. In this overall trade turnover, India's exports to Russia went down from $ 1,640 millions in the 1991-92 to $ 650 millions in 1997-98 and imports also declined from $ 728 millions to $ 500 millions in the same period.[9] From these data it is evident that decline in India's exports to Russia was more significant and sharp as compared to India's imports from Russia during the decade of 1991-2000. Although, India's exports to Russia were more than imports and that India continued to have positive trade balance with Russia during the 1990s the volume of trade balance declined over the years. In other words, India was not able to sustain exports to Russia, while relatively Russia was able to sustain its exports performance to India including defense sales.

So far as commodity composition was concerned, traditional items such as tea, coffee, tobacco, spices continued to be important in India's exports to Russia. At the same time non- – traditional items such as engineering goods lost their significance. However, it is important to note that pharmaceutical products became important in the export basket to Russia. So far as imports from Russia are concerned, ferrous metals, non-ferrous metals, newsprint, continued to be important. But oil, which was a major item of import from Russia to India in the past, declined sharply.

There was no steadiness in trade and wide fluctuations prevailed in trade volume over the years with regard to major commodities such as tea, tobacco, fertilisers, etc. There were several factors that contributed to prevailing trends in India – Russia trade in the 1990s.[10]

1. Firstly, in the first half of the decade, Russia faced crisis conditions of unprecedented proportions. There was sharp decline in the GDP, industrial and agricultural production, break-up of linkages among the republics, etc., which contributed to the general decline in the total foreign trade of Russia. This overall decline in foreign trade of the country also had its effect on India–Russia trade.
2. Secondly, institutions and organisations that prevailed in the Soviet era ceased to exist while new ones were not in place. For example, state monopoly over foreign trade, Central control over regions disappeared, but new institutions to regulate market oriented economy were not in place resulting in uncertainties.
3. Thirdly, as economic transition was still in process, new banking and financial institutions were not fully developed to meet the needs of foreign trade transactions.
4. Fourthly, specific arrangement of Rupee Trade that prevailed in the framework of India–USSR trade was

> discontinued. But by 1993-94 there was multiplicity of trade channels between India and Russia – Debt Repayment Account (DRA); Escrow Account; Hard Currency Account and Unofficial / semi–legal trade channel, which added to the complexities.[11]

The debt issue was resolved and an agreement was reached under which India was to repay Rs 3,000 crores ($ 1 billion) every year in terms of goods to Russia for a period of 12 years starting from 1993-94. In principle this was a rational arrangement considering the fact that the country was in need of basic necessities of life for common man in Russia. But the policy makers and those entrusted with the task of implementation of policies often could not avail of the funds regularly and completely. This was partly because the *modus operandi* of the utlisation of funds was made highly complex with multiplicity of agencies dealing with the allocation and utilisation of funds. The unsatisfactory state of allocation of funds can be had from the fact that there were instances when funds were allocated to sports clubs and even churches, presumably for social and political reasons. But this was not rational to meet the economic needs of the country.

Subsequently, a system of auction of rupee funds was evolved. In some respects this system of auctioning of rupee funds to those organisations engaged in trading with India was more rational. It was claimed that the auctioning of rupee funds was intended to boost the India–Russia trade. It was also observed that the auctioning of rupee funds was often intended to earn much needed funds for the State exchequer. While trading between India and Russia was being conducted, under prevailing circumstances, the system of auction of rupee funds in Russia for importing goods from India was being exploited occasionally by unscrupulous elements, which were keen to take advantage of critical situation in Russia. It appears that there was also no regularity in the auction of rupee funds. Moreover, as observed by some experts there was lack of transparency in the system of auctioning of rupee funds. These shortcomings in the implementation of the policies of the government went against the common interest of promoting healthy trade practices between the two countries. Thus the lack of regularity and transparency in the auctioning of rupee funds partly affected trade. This is evident from the statement by the then Russian Deputy Prime Minister Yuri Yarov that several government agencies were putting up claims on the clearing rupees, which meant that there was no lack of demand for Indian goods to be bought with the clearing rupees.[12]

As a result of these shortcomings, according to banking experts in India often rupee funds got accumulated affecting trade between the two countries. What also added to the problem of trade was that rupee funds were auctioned at a discount of about 20-25 per cent, which amounted to devaluing rupees. This was partly justified on the ground that a Russian importing organisation had to deposit upfront money in Russia for getting clearing rupees funds under the then prevailing conditions of high interest rates of 5-10 per cent per month in Russia.

As observed earlier, there was multiplicity of channels prevailing in the 1990s. But this added to the complexity in trade between India and Russia and it partly affected trade between the two countries. This was evident in the case of major items of India's exports. For instance, export of tea or medicines could be exported to Russia simultaneously through more than one channel by the same or different agencies. As a result of this a consignment of tea exported to Russia was cheaper than a consignment of tea exported under other arrangement. Hard currency trade account was another channel for which there were hardly any restrictions in the India–Russia trade. But in the early 1990s, the quantum of trade for trade from India under this arrangement was not significant. Besides this there was the Escrow Account, under which trade did take place. It appears that the Dollar Escrow Account was gaining importance considering the fact that there was substantial freedom and flexibility in terms of what to import and the destination of supplier and so on.[13]

In addition to these official channels unofficial trade was carried out by fly–by–night operators, which assumed a major proportion in the 1990s.[14] According to some estimates in 1998 unofficial trade amounted to about $ 10 billion. Besides India, Hong Kong, Singapore, Thailand, Turkey, Saudi Arabia were other major countries from which shuttle trade was carried out. This shuttle trade was carried out under abnormal conditions prevailing in Russia and other former Soviet republics. But these fly–by-night operators often traded in substandard goods imported into Russia affecting India's image in the Russian market.

As pointed out earlier, India exported pharmaceutical products to Russia. But there were some issues and complexities involved. For instance, several ministries of the Russian government were involved in the release and use of fund's – Ministry of Finance, Ministry of Health, Ministry of Foreign Economic Relations, etc. Hence as observed by some experts contacting several Russian agencies with all uncertainties had become a task and hence many backdoor dealing with kickbacks continued to persist which affected healthy competition for promoting the India–Russia trade.[15] The release of funds was irregular which created problems for genuine trading firms. It appears that the registration of medicines for Indian firms in Russia was often time consuming. While even leading Indian pharmaceutical firms had to spend five –six months in Russia for the registration of medicines for imports into Russia, firms from the USA and West European countries took a couple of weeks. This put Indian firms at a disadvantage *vis-à-vis* Western firms. Hence, although Russia badly needed medicines and established Indian firms were in a position to supply medicines much cheaper than from the West, some of to point out that some Indian small – scale producers and trading firms adopted unfair promoting trade between the two countries.

Some of these constraints were partly overcome thanks to the initiatives taken by some major Indian pharmaceutical companies and by Russian specialists when Russian importing agencies visited Indian firms and laboratories in the second half of the 1990s. They were convinced about the high quality of Indian medicines as also the competitiveness of these companies in terms of price in the Russian market as compared to Western companies. Such efforts helped India to a great extent to increase the exports of medicines and pharmaceutical products to Russia as also to other Commonwealth of Independent States.[16]

Indo-Russian Trade and Economic Relations since 2000

Indo–Russian economic cooperation has not been commensurate with their mutual potentials. Prof. Felix Yurlov agrees with the opinion of several others that the first ten years of economic relations were a 'lost decade', and a 'decade of lost opportunities'. He says: "Russia, in the mid-1990s, started changing its foreign policy and turning its attention towards east, and India in particular. Time was lost in spite of all advantages which we had in our relations with India, cooperation in different fields like trade and economic field, scientific, military, cultural field. So, we have lost quite a lot in those five years." However, the 2000s witnessed some remarkable developments in bilateral economic cooperation.[17]

Under the Integrated Long-Term Programme of Scientific and Technical Cooperation (ILTP) signed during President Putin's visit to India in October 2000, both countries undertook more than 150 joint scientific projects, which could provide relatively cheap technologies in various fields from biomedicine to semi-conductors, computer chips, new materials and energy sources. During the visit of Indian Petroleum Minister Ram Naik to Moscow in February 2001, the Indian Oil Company, ONGC Videsh Ltd., and the Russian Rosneft signed an agreement on the joint exploration of hydrocarbon resources in the Russian Far-Eastern Island of Sakhalin.[18] During the visit of President Putin to India in December 2002, both sides signed the Joint Declaration on strengthening and developing economic, scientific and technological cooperation. A document on economic cooperation between Indian state of Karnataka and Samara region of Russia, and another document on telecommunication were signed during the visit.

The last quarter of 2003 witnessed some positive developments in economic relations between the two countries. The Confederation of Indian Industry (CII) opened its office at the Russian Chambers of Commerce and Industry in October 2003 to facilitate the process of economic cooperation. During the visit of Prime Minister Vajpayee to Moscow in November 2003, 85 Indian businessmen accompanied him to study the prospects of investments and joint collaborations with Russian companies.[19] Mani Shankar Aiyar, India's Petroleum Minister, visited Moscow in October 2005 to discuss India's energy requirements with Russia. He welcomed Gazprom's (Russian firm) interest in the Iran–Pakistan- India pipeline (IPI). A 10–member high–level delegation of Gazprom arrived in Islamabad in October 2005 to begin formal discussion on the construction of the $7 billion Iran–Pakistan-India (IPI) gas pipeline, and an ambitious project of gas storage in Pakistan. It was the first visit of the Chairman of Gazprom to Pakistan, the world's largest gas producing company with over 20 per cent share in global gas production.[20]

During Prime Minister Manmohan Singh's visit in May 2005, both countries decided to set up a Joint Study Group (JSG) on Economic Cooperation to look into the feasibility of the Comprehensive Economic Cooperation Agreement (CECA).[21] On the Koodankulum issue, the Prime Minister sought to allay fears of President Putin on the nuclear fuel falling into wrong hands and said a bill to prevent its misuse would be introduced in the Indian Parliament. The Indian Cabinet had already okayed the bill. During Manmohan Singh's visit to Moscow in December 2005 to attend the sixth bilateral summit, President Putin said that, "We have been successfully cooperating in nuclear energy and Kudankulam nuclear power project is an example. We see India taking necessary steps to build relations with the Nuclear Suppliers Group (NSG)."[22] Prime Minister Singh observed that there was a vast potential for expansion of cooperation in the field of civil nuclear energy given India's growing energy requirements and the importance of nuclear energy as a clean and viable alternative energy source. Some of the most 'significant and promising areas' of coöperation identified during the visit were energy, telecom and transportation.[23]

A major hurdle in Indo-Russian nuclear cooperation has been the restrictions imposed by Nuclear Suppliers Group (NSG) on both India and Russia. Russia, which is also a member of the 44–member NSG, has assured India of easing the restrictions. Sergei Lavrov, Russia's Foreign Minister during his meeting with External Affairs Minister Natwar Singh in Moscow on 29 October 2005 indicated that NSG could make an exception regarding India in terms of norms observed by the nuclear group so that civilian nuclear energy cooperation could be expanded.[24] Natwar Singh was in Moscow to attend the meetings of the Indo-Russian Inter-Government Commission (IRIGC) and the Shanghai Cooperation Organisations (SCO).

During Prime Minster Singh's visit in 2005, an agreement was signed on technology safeguards while implementing the long-term cooperation in the area of joint development, operation and use of the Russian global navigation satellite system GLONASS. G. Madhavan Nair, Secretary, Department of Space Technology, and A. Perminov, Director, Russian Federal Space Agency, signed the agreement. This agreement envisages launching of GLONASS satellite using GSLV launch vehicle of India. In turn, Russia will provide access to GLONASS system signals for Indian use. It also envisages joint development of user equipment for exploitation of GLONASS signals for commercial purposes. The agreement opens the road for the implementation of a 2004 agreement on joint design and launching of GLONASS communication satellites, which will be used by both countries for civilian and military purposes.[25]

Another agreement on cooperation in the field of solar physics and solar terrestrial relationships within the framework of Coronas–Photon project was signed during the visit. The Coronas–Photon mission aims at research in the field of solar physics and solar terrestrial relationships. The agreement enables integration of the Indian RT-2 payload with the Coronas–Photon spacecraft and the joint space experiment using the RT-2 equipment. The agreement basically revives a Soviet-era Coronas–Photon project under which six instruments fabricated at the Tata Institute of Fundamental Research (TIFR) were to have been installed on a Russian Photon satellite. The project was frozen in the 1990s for lack of funds on the Russian side. During his visit to the Moscow State University, which conferred the title of Professor Honoris Causa, Prime Minister Singh urged the young Russians, especially the entrepreneurs, to visit and invest in India. Speaking before the academic council new face of India", because "There is a need for a new generation of Indians and Russians to discover each other... of late people-to-people, business-to-business contacts have been far below potential and certainly below what our friendship warrants."[26]

Viktor Khristenko, Russia's Energy and Industry Minister, invited India to invest in Russia's energy sector, and join Russian companies in exploration and extraction activities in third countries, particularly in Central Asia. In the context of the interest expressed by ONGC and other Indian companies in picking up a stake in Russian energy companies like Transneft, Manmohan Singh and Khristenko agreed to promote cooperation between their respective oil companies through 'joint ventures and equity participation'.[27] The Russian Minister specifically welcomed India's interest in participating in the Sakhalin-3 oil project in Siberia. India has already invested $2.7 billion in Sakhalin–1, but is expected to have to bargain hard for a share in the even more lucrative Sakhalin-3 venture where Russian and international energy majors such has Lukoil, Gazprom, Rosneft and Exxon Mobil are all jockeying for position. Prime Minister Singh conveyed India's willingness to consider positively the construction of additional reactors in view of its growing energy needs.

In a meeting Prime Minister Singh and Russian businessmen agreed to develop a long-term energy partnership and decided that India and Russia, would explore oil and gas assets both in production and explorations in Third World countries like the Central Asian region. India also responded positively to the Russian request to construct additional nuclear energy is set to play a pivotal role in the India-Russia economic relations since international restrictions on technology transfer to India are expected to be lifted shortly. Referring to India's investment in Sakhalin–I, Manmohan Singh showed interest in Sakhalin–III. The dialogue between ONGC, GAIL, Roseneft and Gazprom, he said, is gaining momentum. Asking the business communities to seize the initiative, the Prime Minister also informed them that India was working on an agreement to permit the utilisation of the remaining rupee debt for Russian investments in India as their bilateral trade was moving from the rupee–rouble arrangements to becoming a fully market determined phenomenon.[28] Both countries discussed the difficult visa regime, lack of information, weak financial base and lack of transport links.

In the field of Indo-Russian economic cooperation, some new areas can be identified. One area is joint cooperation in Central Asia. India could play a bigger role in Russia's energy strategy such as joint exploration and prospecting for new areas in Eastern Siberia and in the Caspian Sea Basin. Involvement in the construction of the pipeline network, modernising and upgradation of existing port facilities is another such area. India will have to go in for long-term agreements to buy Russian oil. The transport route in the present situation is via the Black Sea. A new opportunity that has opened up is to directly deal with the vast regions of Russia. For instance, the agreement between Gujarat and Astrakhan, Karnataka and Samara, can prove helpful. The potential for cooperation in diamond processing, development of inland waterways and road construction needs to be explored.

Both India and Russia have already taken steps such as establishment of ILTP, which currently comprises about 130 projects in 18 thrust areas of science and technology and Intergovernmental Commission on Trade, Economic, Scientific, Technological and Cultural Cooperation, signing of MoU between Confederation of Indian Industry (CII) and Russian Union of Industrialists and Entrepreneurs, India investment in Sakhalin project, the Russian agreement to explore Bay of Bengal, and involvement in Tehri, Barch and Obra power plant projects, etc., to improve bilateral economic relations. The Russian gas sector Gazprom and some of its affiliates such as Stroytransgaz are already working in India, though more synergy needs to be infused in such ventures. India can provide Russia consumer goods such as tea, coffee, tobacco, textiles and some other traditional products. The booming IT industry of India can be another help to Russian economy as it would provide Russian industry the information technology at a comparatively cheaper price than the European counterparts. In the era of globalisation, private sector partnerships must be the new cementing force in Indo-Russian relations.

Russian cooperation with India is phenomenal as some of the recent developments would indicate. When the Indian nuclear power plant at Tarapore went shortage of fuel, the Russian Prime Minister, Fradkov declared Russia's readiness to supply fuel to the hungry nuclear plant at Koodankulam in Tamil Nadu. Russia has agreed to establish 1000 MW nuclear plant at Koodankulam in Tamil Nadu. Russia has also expressed readiness to support Indian move to waive NSG restrictions on India for civil nuclear cooperation. Both the countries are committed to peaceful nuclear cooperation that is mutually advantageous. There are substantial cooperation in the field of defence especially on joint research and development of armaments as in the case of Brahmos. The visit of Indian Prime Minister to EU in 2006 has not been much encouraging from Indian stand point, at least in one respect. The EU, currently led by Finland could not commit the Indian Prime Minister to support India's need to waive NSG restrictions so that India can contact with other countries regarding civil nuclear cooperation. Russia has proved itself different in this context.

Table 1

Russian Export and Import Figures during 2001-06

Values in US Dollars (in million)

	Year					
	2001-02	*2002-03*	*2003-04*	*2004-05*	*2005-06*	*2006-07 (Apr.-Jun.)*
Export	535.51	592.61	659.63	1,322.74	2,022.19	376.45
Total Export	51,413.29	61,412.13	78,149.61	111,517.44	149,165.73	40,935.05
Import	798.18	704.00	713.76	631.26	733.15	181.81
Total Import	43,826.73	52,719.43	63,842.97	83,535.94	103,090.54	29,092.10

Table 1 explains the Russian export and imports with India during the period of 2001-06. The data presented in the above table explains that the trade volume in both export and imports have been increasing at a rapid rate during the period of 2001-06. But it can be noticed that the volume of exports are greater than the imports from India, which signify the advantageous position of Russian in trading with India. For example, the total exports to India were to the tune of US$ 535.51 million and have been increased to US$ 2,022 million in year 2005-06. The growth of imports from India were not grown at the same rate as exports from Russia grew over the period as the total value of imports from India were US$ 798.18 million in year 2001-02 and later shrink to the meagre amount of US$ 181.81 million. Therefore, from the above analysis it could be understood that the though trade relations with Russia are growing but the growth in trade volume is highly advantageous to the Russia than the India.

Table 2

Top 10 Exports to India in 2005-06

Sl.No.	*Commodity*	*2005-06*	*2006-07 (April-June)*
1	Iron and steel	590.09	130.74
2	Fertilisers	484.95	39.19
3	Natural or cultured pearls, precious or semiprecious stones, pre-metals, and jewellery articles	157.20	4.83
4	Nickel and articles thereof	147.01	34.33
5	Paper and paperboard; articles of paper pulp, of paper or of paperboard	100.50	29.30
6	Rubber and articles thereof	80.91	26.53
7	Copper and articles thereof	76.52	21.77
8	Nuclear reactors, boilers, machinery and mechanical appliances; parts thereof	62.70	15.90
9	Organic chemicals	46.11	13.64
10	Salt, sulphur, stone, plastering materials, lime, and cement	41.45	10.80

Values in US$ Million

Table 2 explains the top 10 exports to India from Russia during the period of 2005-06. The data mentioned in the above table explains that iron and steel is the biggest item exported to India, as the total value of export is US$ 590.09 million in year 2005-06. Fertilizers occupies the second position in the top 10 exports to India as the total value of exports is US$ 484.95 million followed by Natural or cultured pearls, precious or semiprecious stones, pre-metals, clad and jewellary articles who net export value is 157.20 million. The export of salt, sulphur, stone, plastering materials, lime, and cement occupies the bottom of the top 10 exports to India as the total export value of these goods is US$ 41.45 million.

Table 3 explains the top 10 exports from India to Russia during the year 2005-06. From the careful analysis of the data presented in the table it could be judged that the pharmaceutical products are the biggest exported goods to Russia as the total export value of pharmaceuticals are US$ 233.15 million in the year 2005-06. The export of coffee, tea, and spice occupies the second biggest export from India to Russia as its net export value is US$ 67.77 million followed by miscellaneous edible preparations worth US$ 54.92 million. The export of electrical machinery and equipment and parts thereof; sound recorders and reproducers, television image and sound recorders and reproducers, and their parts occupies the bottom of the list with 16.79 million during the year 2005-06.

Table 3

Top 10 imports from India in 2005-06

Sl.No.	*Commodity*	*2005-06*	*2006-07 (Apr.–Jun.)*
1	Pharmaceutical products	233.15	59.74
2	Coffee, tea, mate and spice	67.77	14.97
3	Miscellaneous edible preparations	54.92	9.17
4	Tobacco and manufactured tobacco substitutes	39.27	5.72
5	Preparations of vegetables, fruit, nuts or other parts of plants	31.18	4.21
6	Cotton	27.75	6.03
7	Plastic and articles thereof	25.49	4.10
8	Nuclear reactors, boilers, machinery and mechanical appliances; parts thereof	22.67	10.73
9	Articles of apparel and clothing accessories, knitted or crocheted	17.84	10.50
10	Electrical machinery and equipment and parts thereof; sound recorders and reproducers, television image and sound recorders and reproducers, and parts	16.79	5.59

Constraints and Challenges for the Indo-Russian Trade and Economic Relations

The question that now needs to be addressed: what are the factors exactly that arrest economic cooperation between the two countries? Both the countries have huge resources and potential, still the cooperation in trade in 2005 stands about $3.1 billion, several times less that the trade India has with other countries such as the US, China, the UK and Germany. While the total Indian investment in Russia amounts about $2 billion, the Russian investment is about $160 million. Obviously, one major factor is lack of consistent and persuasive political acumen and persistence. The lack of information between the two countries regarding business prospects has acted as a deterrent in this regard. The contentious issues is related to the signing of a likely visa re-admission treaty. Similarly, if there is an invitation then the visa to Indian businessmen to attend business fairs should be immediate and automatic. However, Russia has been demanding that India sign the re-admission treaty with Russia in order to minimise illegal immigrants to Russia via Third World countries. The proposed Russia–India Business Council may work to smoothen and enlighten the prospective business ventures in each other's countries and address issues such as rigid visa regime and bureaucratic problems.[29]

The deficient infrastructure, both geographical and organisation makes the trade relations time consuming and cumbersome. The proposed North- South international transport corridor may help in this context. It represents the shortest route to Europe and Russia. Although, this route is already in use, a major blockade is the Astrakhan customs port. At the moment, they are using an alternative route to Russia not through Bandar Abbas. However the corridor does represent the shortest link to Russia from India. This route needs to be developed for bilateral trade. The Russian and Indian leaders while looking at economic cooperation must respect each other's national interest, and must come out of the old cold war environment and thinking which largely shaped the bilateral economic relations, mainly confined to arms and armaments. The psychological barriers need to be crossed over and this may be redressed to a great extent with the easing of visa restrictions, so that more interactions can take place between the people of both the countries.

The narrow range of traded commodities and high share of raw materials has become one major obstacle in widening the scope of economic cooperation. About 60 per cent of Russia's exports to India fall in four main commodity groups: raw materials, ferrous and non-ferrous metals, fertiliser and news print. There is a need to improve and diversify the commodities range. The proposed Trade and Investment Forum would likely address the issue of lack of investment in each others' countries. Russia has still not decided what to do with the rupee-rouble debt as it could be used to trade and commodities.

There are opportunities for cooperation in the fields of electronics, biotechnology, communications, infrastructure development including construction of highways, ports, airports and metro, extraction and transportation of hydrocarbons, pipe line laying, ferrous and non-ferrous metallurgy and automobile industry. The CII officials argue that problems exist in the way of expanding the potential of trade in the pharmaceutical sector. Registration of products take up to two-three years. By the time registration has been completed, the market scenario changes and producers have to file for new products. Russia follows EU norms for registration, but EU takes a maximum of one year. This gap needs to be addressed by the Russian authorities.

There are some constraints and challenges, which are affecting the trade between the two countries.[30]

1. Firstly, Indian businessmen are often put off by fears of high–risk factor of the Russian market and also the role of mafia elements affecting market environment. While such feelings were relevant about a decade back, situation has substantially changed at present. The Russian economy is growing and vibrant and stable.
2. Secondly, there is a general perception of information Gap about the Russian market conditions, which hampers growth of trade and business –to–business contacts. This is quite genuine since there has been a systemic change in Russian economy. Even information gap about the scope and prospects of Russian market for Indian goods. As stated by Mr. Khemka, there is still a section of businessmen in Russia which feel that India can supply only a few traditional items such a tea, tobacco etc. Hence, there is an urgent need to fill the information gap that prevails in both the countries and disseminate information about the scope and potentialities that exist for trade and

economic cooperation between the two countries including hi-technology areas such as information technology and research in various applied sciences. To some extent this constraincy might be overcome by the opening of the CII office at the Russian Chamber of Commerce and Industry as also the opening of ICICI, State Bank of India and Canara Bank in Russia. Moreover, the growing flow of Indian business delegations to Russia should help in filling the information gap.

3. Thirdly, the problem of long duration and costly transportation of goods from India to Russia has been a major constraint. The opening of North–South Corridor via Iran might partly help in overcoming this problem. This North-South Corridor when fully in operation will not only cut down time but also reduce the cost of transportation of goods to Russia by 15-20 per cent, which will increase competitiveness of India in the Russia market.
4. Fourthly, so far as promoting India's exports to Russia is concerned; a major problem facing Indian exporters is the prevailing cumbersome and difficult visa regime of Russia. It is reported that many businessmen and executives are virtually prevented from visiting Russia to promote trade due to inability to get visa easily and quickly.
5. Fifthly, some Indian business firms suffered huge losses in the 1990s when several Russian banks went on liquidation. Hence, it is reported that this affected the trust in the banking system. However, this problem seems to have been largely overcome to a great extent at present. On the other hand, Russian enterprises and organisations have been able to expand exports of machinery and equipments to India. This is largely because they deal with government and public sector units as in the past. Hence, it may be much easier for them to promote their business transactions in India. Mention may be made of the 1000 MW power units at the Koodankulam Nuclear Plant in Tamil Nadu, Tehri Hydropower Plant Mashniy Company supplies India with energy facilities for seven projects, Tekhnopromexport delivers equipment to two construction sites. Similarly, Russian organisations such as

Gazprom, Tyazpromexport provide equipments for modernisation of energy, metallurgical and chemical industrial units in India.[31]

Prospects of Indo-Russian Trade and Economic Relations

Prospects of the India–Russia economic ties are quite good. The present level of trade between the two countries is far below the potentialities. Firstly, both India and Russia are large countries with expanding economies. GDP growth in both the countries has been in the range of 6-8 per cent during the last few years and this growth has been sustained. Secondly, at present both Russia and India have huge hard currency reserves of $ 270 billion and $ 190 billion respectively, which indicted vast market opportunities and scope for the development of a wide range of economic sectors without much resource constraints. Thirdly, there is sustained goodwill and interest between the two countries to promote sincerely economic ties. This is evident from various initiatives taken by the leaders of both the countries in terms of holding summit meetings regularly, setting up of Joint Study Group (JSG) to examine the feasibility of a Comprehensive Economic Cooperation Agreement (CECA), arranging exhibitions from time to time in both the counties. Presumably for these reasons India and Russia have set trade turnover target of $ 10 billion by 2010. But considering the fact that the present level of trade turnover is about $ 2 billion, a rise of about five times appears to be rather ambitious. Hence this is a challenge for the leadership of both the countries to translate declarations into reality. Fourthly, according to some experts in the pharmaceutical sector, there are good prospects for Russian chemical companies to supply chemicals and raw materials to Indian bulk drug manufacturers, which are engaged in producing medicines to world market.

Fifthly, there is good scope for promoting cooperation in hi-technology area such as information technology, biotechnology, etc. The president of Russia, Mr. Vladimir Putin, mentioned about it more than once during the last five-six years. Sixthly, efforts have already been made to establish friendship and cooperation between regions and cities in Russia and India such as Gujarat and Astrakhan, Karnataka and Samara region, Andhra and Tatarastan,

Mumbai and St. Petersburg and so on. This form of cooperation should go beyond the formal exchange of social and political visits and should result in business interaction and exchange of information and contacts and proposals in terms of trade economic joint ventures. In connection with promoting the India Russia trade, it is stated by Nand Khemka of the FICCI, New Delhi in February 2007, "One of the prime needs for both the countries is to enhance economic co-operation and correct the balance between the trades as well as to promote engagement in different value chains."[32]

Given the geographical distance between India and Russia, India cannot hope to take China's place in terms of volume of bilateral trade, currently pegged at $29.1 billion in 2005, up 37.1 per cent year on year. However, India and Russia can boost greater cooperation in diverse fields through joint ventures, collaborations and joint development initiatives. A major area of synergy between India and Russia is in the energy sector. Russia's importance as a supplier of energy feeds into India's own rising demand for multiple sources of energy to fuel its growing economy.

The following are the major areas identified by the Confederation of Indian Industry (CII) during its interactions with Russian delegation in January 2007.[33]

Pharmaceuticals: Russia is the second largest export destination for Indian pharmaceutical products, after the United State. However, while the US market is witnessing a negative growth, Indian exports to Russia have witnessed a 42 per cent growth. India's ranking in Russia's market has fallen from secondposition to fifth, after France, Germany, Slovenia and Hungary. A McKinsey report suggests that India's pharma market will rise to US$ 25 billion by 2010, of which US$ 11 billion will consist of domestic sales. India is competitive in terms of production costs, setting up plants (it is 40 per cent cheaper to set up plants in India) and clinical research (35 per cent to 40 per cent savings in conducting research in India). Russia is the eighth largest pharma market and the ninth largest generic market in the world. Also, Russian demands for pharma products are rising as cardiovascular, respiratory, cerebrovascu diseases are increasing.

Energy: Indian and Russian companies can expand collaborations and joint ventures in third countries in the energy sector. The security of supply and the security of demand will lead to a stable partnership. India has already invested $2.7 billion in Sakhalin–1 but is expected to have to bargain hard for a share in the even more lucrative Sakhalin-3 venture where Russian and international energy majors such as Lukoil, Gazprom, Rosneft and Exxon Mobil are all jockeying for position. India's energy needs can substantially met by the Russian reserve in oil and natural gas.

Prospects of cooperation in third Countries: particularly in Central Asia. Both counties could invest in coal/iron ore and the mining sectors. During Prime Minister Manmohan Singh's visit to Moscow in 2005, both the countries agreed to explore oil and gas assets both in production and explorations in Third World countries like the Central Asian region.

High technology: Cooperation with Russia is another area that India should keep pushing for such as in the area of coal gasification. A technology centre is proposed to be set up in Moscow that will help Indian companies to transform their ideas from the lab into a profitable business.

Financial services: The network of Russian banks is very underdeveloped in India, and even though there are some Indian banks in Russia, much still needs to be done. The CII has already opened its office at the Russian Chambers of Commerce and Industry in October 2003 to facilitate the process of economic cooperation. The Russia–India Business Council may work to smoothen and enlighten the prospective business ventures in each other's countries and address issues such as rigid visa regime and bureaucratic problems. The council would likely open new avenues of cooperation among the business communities of the two countries.

Research and development and the commercialisation of technology: both countries can cooperate in this area. The real estate sector, Infrastructure, energy and machinery are some of the main sectors that the Russian side can invest in India. Hyper-mechanical equipment is needed by India. There is also scope for cooperation in areas like mining sector, textiles, particularly synthetic fibres, etc. Projects such as expansion of air links between Indian and Russia can also be undertaken. The announcement in 2006 of direct flight from Amritsar to Moscow is one such step that would enable more accessibility, especially to the businessmen from Punjab to Russia and vice versa.

Conclusion

More concrete steps need to be taken to boost Indo-Russian economic relations. It is true that when the spirit of political bonhomie is infused to economic sphere, the two countries would most likely touch bilateral trade to the tune of $10 billion by the year 2010. Though, some of the Western analysts fear that under the current dispensation led by Vladimir Putin, a full transformation to market economy is improbable. India needs not be worried about those predictions. It is true that the economic cooperation between the two countries is not commensurate with their bilateral political and strategic cooperation, but it is nonetheless commendable that both the countries have made remarkable progress in this area. Besides sharing common concerns and cooperation in the areas of counter–terrorism, multipolar global structure, conflicts in Chechnya and Kashmir, the coming years would likely witness rapid developments in bilateral economic cooperation.

As a result of these changes, the current bilateral trade is based on payments in freely convertible currencies. All Russian exports to India follow the new system. But in the last decade, about two third of Indian exports were financed through the renegotiated rupee-debt repayment mechanism. As a result of all these economic policy changes, traditional actors in Indo-Russian trade and other economic relations like the public sector units and state trading corporations are no longer as relevant as they used to be in the Soviet era. Sections of Indian private sector, which used to get away with selling many products of questionable quality under the bilateral system, also found it difficult to adjust to radically changed economic and commercial environment in Russia, driven by market forces.

The Indo-Russian economic cooperation is on the rise. According to the Vice-Premier of Russian Federation Zhukov, Moscow hopes to increase bilateral trade to the annual level estimated by $10 billion in the nearest years. By investing into the leading Indian economy branch of high technologies, and by controlling country's power market, Moscow acquired an opportunity to amplify its influence on Indian foreign policy. The transport South - North corridor, which connects India with the EU through Russia and Iran, will, most likely, lead to the decrease of the share of Indo-American trade in total New Delhi's import-export balance. And inevitably this will affect the entire mutual relations between New Delhi and Washington. Besides, due to ITC Russia created conditions for appearance of the powerful South Asian economic alliance (India-Iran), which can include other countries of the region. Together with the other above mentioned levers of pressure, and by means of military - technological cooperation with India, Russia sets up preconditions leading to the decrease of the American presence (including military) in the Indian Ocean region in the twenty-first century. Significant strengthening of the Russian influence in the South Asia achieved through all these means, may lead to the reviving of the Soviet idea of creation of a powerful triple Russia-India–China alliance.

References

1. Hannes Adomeit, "Russia as 'great power" in *World Affairs: Iimages and Reality,"International Affairs,* Vol. 71, No.1, January, 1995, p.44.
2. Ibid., p.45.
3. http://www.pbs.org/newshour/bb/europe/july-dec98/russia_7-13.html
4. http://www.jamestown.org/publications_details.php?volume_id=5&issue_id=293&article_id=3285
5. Ibid.
6. Excerpt from the speech of Boris Yelstin, President of the Russian Federation in the Central Hall of Parliament on 29 January 1993, in *Strategic Digest,* Vol. 23, No.4, April 1993, p. 592.
7. *National Herald,* 26 October, 1996.
8. Ibid.
9. *National Herald,* 10 October 1996.
10. http://www.theglobeandmail.com/servlet/story/RTGAM.20040212.wsovi0212/BNPrint/Front.
11. Ibid.
12. Ibid.

13. *News Time,* 17 February 1996.
14. *National Herald,* 15 March 1997.
15. Ibid.
16. *The Hindustan Times,* 24 March 1997.
17. Personal Interview with Felix Yorlov, Professor and Head, Modern Studies Department, Institute of Oriental Studies , Washington, U.S.A. on 5 December 2003.
18. *Strategic Digest,* Vol. 32, No.12, December 2002, pp. 1430-32.
19. *The Hindu,* 10 November, 2003.
20. Ibid.
21. *The Tribune,* 8 October 2005.
22. Ibid.
23. Ibid.
24. *The Kashmir Times,* 10 May 2005.
25. *Daily Excelsior,* 7 December 2005.
26. *The Tribune,* 20 October 2005.
27. *The Pioneer,* 6 December 2005.
28. *The Hindu,* 6 December 2005.
29. Nivedita Das Kundu, on "Indo-Russian Relations: An Overview", available at http://www.helsinki.fi/aleksanteri/english/publications /ap_das_ kundu.htm,
30. http://www.pbs.org/newshour/bb/europe/july-dec98/russia_7-13.html.
31. Ibid.
32. http://lcweb2.loc.gov/cgibin/query/r?frd/cstdy:@field(DOCID+ru0119).
33. Ibid.

4

Indo-Russian Defence and Military Relations during Post-ColdWar Period (1991-2003)

Introduction

India and Russia enjoyed a close strategic relationship during the duration of the cold war. The relationship was a comprehensive one embracing political, military, cultural and economic cooperation and exchanges. Initially, the US tried to co-opt India as a major partner in the South Asian subcontinent, and extended official invitation to the Indian Prime Minister, Jawaharlal Nehru, to visit USA, who did pay a visit to the US in 1949. However, under Mr. Nehru's purported role of being a fully independent and a non-aligned leader, India in the Korean war in the 1950s, gave unstinted support for China during the early 1950s, and was unwilling to align itself with the US in the latter's attempt to counter and contain the communist threat emanating from China and the Soviet Union, which then distanced it from the US. Moreover, Nehru's visit to Peking in 1954, and his acceptance of the Soviet invitation to go to the Soviet Union ultimately turned the US attention towards its neighbour Pakistan, which was destined to play a major role as the 'most allied ally' of the US in the Asian region.[1] This backdrop of the developing Pakistan-US relations helped both the Soviet Union and India in coming together for strategic reasons. This chapter attempts to analyse the basis for the establishment of Soviet-India strategic relationship during the cold war, and its culmination into the Treaty of Peace, Friendship and Cooperation in 1971. It also focuses on the post-cold war relations between the two countries, especially the ongoing military-technical cooperation between India and the successor state of Russia.

Indo-Soviet Strategic Relations during the Cold War

The history of Indo-Soviet relations can be described as a friendship purely based on Indian needs, Soviet opportunism, and Western ambivalence. Despite their differing philosophies and political and social systems, the two countries cooperated closely throughout the cold war era. South Asia has always occupied a central place in Soviet diplomacy. Since the end of the Second World War, most of the Soviet aid and political endeavours were concerned with Asia and other parts of the Third World. Initially, the Soviet Union was lukewarm towards India for which two factors could be cited. India's decision in April 1949, to remain within the Commonwealth, in contravention to its past declarations of abhorrence towards the Western world, and Indian Prime Minister, Jawaharlal Nehru's, announcement on May 7, 1949, that he had accepted an invitation to visit the United States in October of that year.

However, things took a different turn when on February 25, 1954, US President Eisenhower announced his government's decision to provide arms to Pakistan. A month later, Pakistan and the US signed a mutual defence assistance agreement.[2] Some four months later, Pakistan joined the US sponsored military pact, the SEATO, and subsequently the CENTO in 1955. This agreement brought a radical change in South Asia, for these agreements assured Pakistan the supply of sophisticated military hardware and economic aid in larger quantity from a superpower.

The new situation alarmed New Delhi, which, since its independence, was envisaging a greater regional role, if not a global one, for itself. Its obstinacy in solving the Kashmir dispute with Pakistan, and later with China over northeastern Ladakh and the Aksai Chin of the Kashmir state and over the McMohan line, which demarcates the eastern border of China and India, had forced the regional countries to look towards India with suspicion. The situation forced New Delhi to undertake an expansion of its military establishment and to find ways and means of offsetting the additional diplomatic strength gained by Pakistan. It also provided Moscow with an opportunity to develop its relations with New Delhi, since Soviet Union could not tolerate the US presence in its backyard. Such a political line was understandable, since India with her big size and strategic location was politically stable and industrially more developed than the other countries of the region. Furthermore, the USSR could use India's status as a leader of the Non-aligned Movement to bolster Soviet policy in the Third World. Thus, a closer cooperation with India could make it relatively easier for the Soviet Union to forestall the influence of unfriendly major powers in the area. India and the Soviet Union, therefore, tended to pursue similar policies by holding that US military aid to Pakistan increased tension in South Asia. Against this background, India and Soviet Union exchanged military Attaches, who were assigned their respective positions in the embassies in Moscow and New Delhi.[3]

However, it was when the Sino-Soviet and Sino-Indian relations began to deteriorate in 1959-1960, that the Soviets began investing in military aid to India, to enable it to stand up to the People's Republic of China, and to prop up an influential India to counter any Chinese influence in the region. The other motive behind this was to maintain the balance of power in the area, and to offset the Pakistan-China strategic nexus, which had started to develop following Sino-Indian War of 1962.

On September 11, 1964, an agreement was signed between India and the USSR, under which Moscow agreed to give India three squadrons of MiG-21 aircraft, 170 tanks, and 20 helicopters. The purchases were to be paid for in Indian rupees over ten years at a 2 per cent interest. India also took advantage of the Soviet and US growing apprehensions regarding China, and received economic aid from the Western world, particularly the USA. By 1967, India had received approximately US $ 7.25 billion of non-military foreign grants and credits from the American government. The country also began to receive military assistance in 1962, following the Sino-Indian border conflict, but the precise amount is to date 'classified'.[4]

However, during the Indo-Pakistan war of 1965, Western embargo on the shipment of weapons to India and Pakistan made New Delhi almost wholly dependent on Moscow for the supply of sophisticated weapons in the years to come. Thus, the Soviet

Union became the major source of economic and military assistance for India. By the end of the cold war, that the Indian forces were highly dependent on the supply of Soviet arms and armaments, can be gauged from the fact that by early 1990s, at the time of demise of the Soviet Union, the reliance of Indian forces was to the extent of: Army 75 per cent, Air Force 80 per cent, and Navy 85 per cent.[5]

In March 1969, armed clashes between the Soviet Union and China at the Ussuri River along the northern borders further worsened the Sino-Soviet relations. In these circumstances, Moscow needed India's cooperation as much as New Delhi needed it. However, it was the Sino-American rapprochement in 1970, which India thought of as upsetting the military equation in the subcontinent. This prompted Russia and India to sign a Twenty Years Treaty of Peace, Friendship and Cooperation on August 9, 1971.

The peak point of the IndoSoviet relations was reached when the two countries signed the 'Treaty of Peace, Friendship and Cooperation on August 9, 1971. Although, the treaty was stated to be a political one, with emphasis on promotion of "consolidation of universal peace and security, preservation and strengthening of peace in Asia and throughout the world, halting of arms race, complete disarmament, elimination of colonialism and racism, and respect for India's non-alignment policy", it sounded more as a military alliance to counter China and Pakistan in particular, and the US in general. This can be gauged from the fact that, Article IX of the treaty stated that the parties undertake to abstain from providing any assistance to any third party that engages in armed conflict with the other party. In the event of either party being subjected to an attack or a threat thereof, the parties shall immediately enter into mutual consultations in order to remove such threats and to take appropriate effective measures to ensure peace and the security of their countries.[6]

In consonance with this Treaty, the Soviet Union began to strengthen India's defence capabilities, and when called upon to live up to their treaty obligations, during the third India-Pakistan war soon after in December 1971, lent both material and diplomatic support to India. The Soviet Union played a decisive role in the dismemberment of the East Pakistan, both at the

Security Council and in the military assistance it rendered to India. It vetoed the Peking-supported US resolution in the Security Council on December 5, 1971, which called for the immediate cessation of hostilities, the withdrawal of the armed forces, and stationing of observers on the India-Pakistan border. To the contrary, Soviet Union, in line with the Indian stand, demanded first for a political settlement in East Pakistan, to be followed by a cessation of hostilities.

On December 6, 1971, the Soviet Union vetoed another resolution supported by the US, in which the Soviet Union's recommendations did not contain any reference to a 'political settlement' of the East Pakistan crisis as a priority. Along with eight other socialist countries, the Soviet Union once more vetoed an Argentine-sponsored resolution asking for the cessation of hostilities and withdrawal of armed forces from each other's territory.

On December 13, it used its veto for the third time to prevent the passage of a US resolution calling for an immediate ceasefire. To the contrary, it supported the Polish resolution, which urged Pakistan to take steps for a peaceful transfer of power in the 'eastern theatre of conflict' to the lawfully elected representatives of the people, headed by Sheikh Mujibur Rehman,[7] as the 'correct approach'. Pakistan construed the Soviet stand as interference in its internal affairs.[6] The Indians paid in kind when it kept a deafening silence over the Soviet Union's invasion of Afghanistan in December 1979, at a time when international efforts were being consolidated to secure its withdrawal. In fact, India continued to cooperate with the illegitimate communist governments of Babrak Karmal and later Dr. Najeebullah in Afghanistan. India even participated in the 1980 Olympics held in the Soviet Union, which were boycotted by major countries of the world to express their resentment over the Soviet Union's action.

The insidious nature of the treaty can further be gauged from the fact that at the time of the ratification of the treaty by the Presidium of the USSR Supreme Soviet, the then USSR Foreign Minister, Andrei Gromyko, stated that from then on, "no one can frame his policy, whether towards the Soviet Union or India, without taking this Treaty into consideration".[8]

The special relationship enjoyed by both the countries, however, started diluting when Gorbachev came into power in the Soviet Union, and set in motion the paradigm switch towards China as well as towards the Prestroika policies internally. He started calling for 'a new China policy', and 'an end to China encirclement policy'.[9] Thus, the mainstay of India-Russia strategic partnership and the Indo-Soviet Peace and Friendship Treaty of 1971, aimed at an encirclement of China, seemed to be quickly waning.

Russo-Indian Military Collaboration in the Post-Cold War Era

With the disintegration of the Soviet Union in December 1991, its successor Russia was faced with three broad, and partially overlapping, geostrategic options, related to the country's national interests and its status *vis-à-vis* America. It is generally agreed that in the post-Soviet Russia, there were divergent opinions on foreign policy making among the Russian Foreign Ministry, the academic community and the parliamentary circles. In the initial period around 1992-1995, the Westerners, or the 'Atlantists' group, led by Andrei Kozyrev, the first Foreign Minister of the post-Soviet Russia, and his foreign policy establishment was in clear ascendance. Thus, in this period, Asia in general and South Asia in particular was accorded a low priority in Moscow's domestic restructuring. In January 1993, the Russian Foreign Ministry published the 'Concept of Russian Federation's Foreign Policy', in which South Asia was accorded the seventh place in its list of ten priorities.[10] The emphasis was on 'Look West' policy, emphasising close relations with the Western European countries. This was due to the fact that Russian leaders appeared to reset their hopes for a rejuvenation of the Russian economy on inputs of massive economic aid from the West. However, this could not materialise to the optimum, since the West still remained suspicious of Russia and the tremendous amount of corruption and disorganisation within Russia's bureaucracy curtailed the potential effectiveness of the Western financial assistance that was in fact given

The main sufferer of this restructuring policy was India, which in the preceding decade had also witnessed a rapidly galloping Russia-China relationship in the making, especially in strategic spheres. Concurrent with this was the growing cold-shouldering of India by Russia, especially between 1989 and 1996, after Primakov became the Prime Minister in 1996. President Boris Yelstin, while adopting a policy of building up a 'strategic relationship of coalition with China,' empahsised the need for 'a de-ideologisation of its (Russia's) foreign policy', which resulted in Russia adopting a 'wait and see' policy towards India, and which led to placing the Indo-Russia relations in a precarious position in the new Russia.[11]

Against this backdrop, India's hegemonistic designs suffered tremendously. India, which viewed itself as a rising regional actor, its military power being one element in this process, had lost a potential partner in order to achieve its ambitious military aspirations. The primary, short-term, military concern for India, in the early 1990s, was to ensure limited supply of spare parts of the Soviet-produced armament. The break-up of the Soviet Union had caused a fracture in the Soviet-Indian military supply-line, due to which India's military faced an immediate crisis. Moreover, India, in response to its economic crisis in 1990-91, and the temporary loss of its primary foreign arms supplier, imposed a reduction in defence expenditure and a sharp reduction in arms imports. After having been the top importer of conventional weapons in the world during the period from 1988 to 1992, India ranked as the twenty-third largest importer of conventional arms by 1996. Meanwhile, Russia's share of the global arms market also dropped from 32 per cent in 1989 to 8 per cent in 1994. The inability of Russia to continue the earlier Soviet flow of military hardware, coupled with the sharp reduction in Indian military expenditure, weakened the primary bond that had united India and the Soviet Union during the cold war.[12]

The visit of President Boris Yelstin to India in January 1993, to an extent helped to assurage Indian resentment towards Russia and helped in the development of bilateral relations. During the visit, the two sides signed a fundamental document. The Treaty of Peace, Friendship and Cooperation, which amounted to a furtherance of the 1971 Soviet Indian Treaty of Peace Friendship and Cooperation.

By the mid-1990s, however, the recovery of Indian economy and the financial needs of Russia's military-industrial complex quickly mended the temporary 'hiccup' in Russo-Indian military cooperation. Further developments took place in November 1996, when India signed an ambitious US $1.8 billion deal with Russia to purchase 40 Sukhoi SU-30 MKI, multi-role aircraft with mid-air refueling capability. New beginnings in their relationship started when in December 1998, a two-day summit was attended by Russian Prime Minister, Yevgeny Primakov, and Indian Prime Minister Atal Behari Vajpayee and other government and opposition leaders in New Delhi. An arms deal was also clinched in which Russia agreed to sell another 10 SU-30K to India. They also announced that the following year they would sign a strategic partnership pact, and also double the bilateral trade by the year 2000.[13]

A major breakthrough was achieved in Indo-Russia relations, when Russian President, Vladimir Putin, visited India in October 2000 and signed a 'Declaration on Strategic Partnership'. The Declaration stated that the two parties sought "to impart a qualitatively new character and long-term perspective to their multifaceted bilateral relations and to actively develop them in political, economic, trade, scientific, technological, cultural and other fields, in the years ahead and into the 21st Century." The declaration specifically spoke of 'consolidating the defence and military-technical cooperation in a long-term perspective, and deepening service-to-service cooperation'. Regarding political cooperation, it spoke of "joint initiatives on key international and regional issues; informing each other of planned foreign policy initiatives in the international arena."[14] The two countries also signed a defence accord that envisaged creating an Indo-Russian Commission on Military-Technical Cooperation.

Analysing the Treaty, one comes to the conclusion that the most significant part of it, perhaps, was the signing of several multimillion-dollar arms contracts. Moreover, arms sales agreement also provided for joint production and development of new generation arms and complete transfer of technology. Moreover, both India and Russia stated that their strategic partnership was not aimed against any third country. Observers, however, said that it could nevertheless be interpreted as a warning for countries not friendly towards India, like Pakistan. Since then, both countries have taken a tough stand and committed themselves to fight against international terrorism, and both have stressed the dangers represented by Islamic fundamentalism. This seems to be a direct reference to the Pakistan military regime and Afghanistan's Taliban role in allegedly sponsoring terrorism in India. It is significant to quote here the remarks of Russian President, Vladimir Putin, while addressing the Indian Parliament, when he said that the same forces were carrying out terrorist attacks "from the Philippines to Kosovo, including Kashmir and Russia's North Caucasus."[15] Prime Minister Vajpayee said that they would forge a coordinated strategy to In the post-cold war era, the revival of Indo-Russian partnership and their growing military ties now seems to be driven more by Indian military needs and political opportunism, like its desire for a permanent seat in the UN Security Council, and Russia's economic needs. Russia is trying to create geo-political stability in the world by challenging Washington's unilateral and independent actions in world affairs, by striving to co-opt India and China. Former Russian Prime Minister Primakov called for an expanded 'strategic triangle' in Asia that would involve China.[16] But China responded with a terse rejection, thereby stressing an independent position, while India also expressed indifference to that Soviet offer.

India's broader strategic goals mean that it is pursuing an ambitious modernisation programme across all of its armed forces. The plan is to spend some US $ 95 billion over the next 15 years. The current level of Russo-Indian collaboration has three facets:(1) acquisition of sophisticated and most modern weaponry from Russia; (2) upgradation of its obsolete weapons earlier provided by the Soviet Union during the cold war; (3) efforts on transfer of technology or joint research and production of latest hi-tech weaponry is also being pursued vigorously, so as to attain self-sufficiency in arms production. It seems that, so far, India has been successful in initiating the initial phases of the above mentioned goals.[17]

It is pertinent to mention here that in the last five years, i.e., 1996-2001, Indian defence forces have spent nearly US $ 5 billion on defence acquisition programmes. Furthermore, by the end of the year 2007, India is poised to spend an estimated US $ 22.22 billion on defence acquisitions. Many defence acquisition programmes are in the pipeline – such as the acquisition of 66 Hawk 100 Advance Jet Trainers (AJT), at a cost of US $1.2 billion; one or two Airborne Warning And Control Systems (AWACS) aircraft; 300 115mm Howitzer self-propelled guns for the Indian Army; weapon-locating radar; lease of a nuclear submarine for the Navy; electronic warfare equipment; and acquisition of an aircraft carrier. The following section gives details of some of the military acquisitions, sale and transfer of technology by Russia to India.[18]

Indian Army

One of the major deals signed between the two in the post-cold war period was the sale of 320 T-90 tanks, worth US $ 700 million by Russia to India. The deal signed in October 2000, during the Russian President, Vladimir Putin's visit to India will enhance India's defence capability to a great extent. The tank, being the latest and sophisticated of its kind, is an advanced version of the T-72 MBT. Along with other accessories, the tank is equipped with laser-guided missiles with a range of five kilometres, a laser range finder coupled with the new gunner's thermal sight, which permits the tank to engage targets while on the move and at night.

The deal also provided for transfer of technology and manufacture of both T-90 MBT and the weapon systems fitted on board. Of the 310 T-90 tanks that are being initially purchased, 124 will be in a ready-for-use configuration, while the remaining tanks will be produced under license in India at the Indian Heavy Vehicle Factory, Avadi.[19]

This tank deal has been signed in the backdrop of India's doctrinal preference to fight its future wars in the deserts, rather than in the mountains of Kashmir, or the riverine terrain of Punjab.

According to the Indian military strategists, deserts offer the opportunity of launching rapid thrust by mechanised columns, spearheaded by tanks, offensive sweeps, in turn, facilitate the subjection of key command and control centres as well as strategic roads. In case of a war with Pakistan, the Indian Army is likely to quickly advance in the Thar Desert area towards the communication nodes around Rahimyar Khan.[20]

Moreover, Russia in line with India's order placed on August 2000, also decided to provide India with powerful laser-guided Krasnopol artillery shells especially designed by Russian Instrument Design Bureau, the KBP, for India's Bofors guns, in a bid to improve its range and pinpoint accuracy of these guns. The induction of this precision-guided munitions by the Indian artillery force in high altitude area of 4500 metres and above, will greatly enhance the capability of the Indian artillery regiments deployed along the volatile Line of Control. The high-accuracy guided projectiles have the ability to hit targets, which include bunkers, vehicles or Kashmari Mujahideen's hideouts, without the risk of collateral damage. It would also enable the artillery to target armoured vehicles moving along mountain roads.[21]

Meanwhile, it was also reported that Russia is providing India a prototype artillery fire-control system earlier conceived in 1995 and which was to be tested in October 2001. The project, Artillery Combat Command and Control System (ACCCS) worth US $ 500 million, intends to upgrade India's land combat command and control networks, and to tie together headquarters, sensors, guns and even helicopters to marshal a fivefold increase in effective firepower.[22]

Indian Air Force

It is generally believed nowadays that air power will be a decisive factor in any future conflicts. Future wars will start with air power and defeat and victory will be decided when either side concedes defeat in the air. In line with this widely held belief, the Indian Air Force has embarked on a three-prong effort: to purchase highly sophisticated and competitive combat aircraft; upgradation of the existing fighter aircraft to make them highly effective for the decades to come; and to stress upon the indigenous production of effective aircraft.

The Indian Air Force (IAF) has, therefore, drawn up a 'Vision Plan of Indian Air Force-2020'.[23] Under this plan, IAF has shifted its emphasis from defensive to offensive capability, and strives to acquire 20 squadrons of multi-role aircraft during the next 15 to 20 years, in addition to the 39 squadrons it currently has. The plan, worth US $ 25 billion, takes into account perceived threats from adjacent Pakistan as well as China, and calls for purchasing:

- 350 multi-role aircraft.
- Early warning and surveillance aircraft such as the Israel-made Fhalcons.
- Refueling aircraft.
- Unmanned aerial vehicles.
- Helicopters and other air assets.[24]

The former Chief of Air Staff, Air Chief Marshal Anil Yashwant Tipnis, once had said that the Indian Air Force wanted to upgrade its fleet with purchases of fighters such as the Russian SU-30MKI, the French Mirage 2000 and British Hawk trainer aircraft. Besides signing agreements with Russia in October 2000 to produce SU-30MKI, India has also received sales offer by the French Aircraft Dassault for its standard-version Rafale, which can carry atomic weapons, and has a long range. Moreover, ten Mirage 2000s from Dassault were ordered in September 2000.[25]

Currently, Russia is involved in the up-gradation of India's 125 MiG-21b is aircraft. Under the agreement worth US $ 312 million, signed in March 1996, two planes had already been upgraded in Russia, and the rest are to be upgraded at Hindustan Aeronautics Limited (HAL) by the year 2004, for which Russia will provide the technical know-how and the kits. Both Russia and India claim that the upgraded planes will have the capabilities of fourth generation aircraft. It was also reported that about 298 combat aircraft would be upgraded in the next 10 years, for which about US $ 312.5 million would be spent on refurbishing 125 Mig-21bis, while US $ 450 million and US $ 300 million would be spent on the upgradation of 120 MiG-27Ms and 45 MiG-29 respectively. Moreover, it was reported that India and Russia are also negotiating licensed production of Phazotron-NIIIR Kopyo radar—the main item in the upgradation of the MiG-21bis, and also for the modernisation of the IAF's Mig-29UB, and MiG-AT.[26]

India and Russia signed a deal worth US $170 million in the year 2000 in New Delhi, for the supply of 40 advanced version of Mi-17-1B helicopters, which can be used both for attack and transport roles in high altitude areas. The IAF wanted to deploy the helicopters in Kargil and Siachen sectors by the end of 2001. The Mi-17 will give a decisive edge to the IAF once they are armed with 12 Vikr-M (AT-16) medium-range, air-to-surface missiles with capabilities to destroy ground based targets. The strike power of the IAF will get tremendous boost in high altitude areas with the laser-guided weapons with a capability of destroying targets within a range of 10 km. Besides, modifications of some of the Indian Mi-8s helicopters had already taken place with Russian engineers working in India for their refurbishment. Moreover, Russia will also deliver 12 Ka-31 helicopters to India for deployment on aircraft carrier, Admiral Gorshkov, currently under refurbishment in Russia, and to be delivered to India in the year 2004-2005.

On December 28, 2001, India and Russia took their relations far beyond a buyer-seller relationship to one based on joint research and production, when they signed their largest defence deal for the production of 140 Sukhoi SU-30MKI multi-role jets in India by Hindustan Aeronautics Limited (HAL), over a span of 17 years. Under the deal, India would be given a license which provides for the indigenous production of all components of SU-30 MKI, including state-of-the-art thrust vectoring engines. This technology could also be utilised by India in the production of its Light Combat Aircraft (LCA). Commenting about the SU-30MKI, a German defence journal, the Military Technology writes that "of particular interest and significance ... is the Indian SU-30MKI version, which integrates various avionics equipment of Russian, French, Israeli and local origin; ... the final and complete configuration promises to be possibly the most capable long-range, multi-role fighter-bomber in existence anywhere in the world."[27]

Apart from this, an earlier deal was signed in December 1998, for the purchase of 10 SU-K, which would be finally upgraded to the MKI standard. Under an earlier US $1.8 billion Sukhoi deal signed in November 1996 with Russia, India will get 40 SU-30MKI multi-role fighters with mid-air refueling capability. A batch of first ten SU-30MKI will be delivered by the end of 2001, and 32 more will be supplied to India by the end of 2003.[28] Moreover, Russia has also expressed its willingness to jointly develop a fifth generation combat fighter, Berkut S-37 with India. When materialised, the plane will be developed in India, and would be used by both the Russian and Indian Airforces. Moreover, In January 2001, the Russian Deputy Prime Minister, Ilya Klebanov, also expressed his immense interest to be involved in the joint production of the Light Combat Aircraft (LCA).[29] It has also been agreed between Moscow and India to open a spare parts and services centre in India to provide spares, overhaul and maintenance for Russian fighter jets supplied to India. The Russian government will soon issue a decree about opening the centre, negotiations for which have been going on for sometime between Russia's Aerospace Equipment Corporation (AEC) and Hindustan Aeronautics Limited (HAL). This will improve the generally slow level of Russian after-sales support, maintenance and provision of spare parts to India and other countries.[30]

During the session of Indo-Russian Joint Commission on Military-Technical Cooperation in June 2001, Russia's Deputy Prime Minister, Ilya Klebanov, offered to build an integrated air defence system for India that can defend against attack by either aircraft or missiles. Calling the system large and very complicated, he suggested that it would provide air defence coverage for all of India. Russia and India are also planning to jointly design and develop a 100-seater, multi-role aircraft. In this connection, Hindustan Aeronautics Limited (HAL) and Russia's Irkutsk Aviation Industrial Association have already joined hands in this US $ 650 million dollar project. The plane was expected to be in the market by 2007.[31]

Moreover, it is also reported that under the defence cooperation protocol worth US $10 billion, signed in June 2001, Russia had proposed to offer India an export variant of the Myasishchev Design Bureau's M-55RTR (NATO reporting name: 'Mystic-B') high altitude reconnaissance aircraft. The proposal would see India pay the US $ 150 million as cost of building and testing the plane. The plane, apart from being equipped with other sophisticated technology, is also used to detect ballistic missile launches. The Mystic-B airframe is capable of operating at altitudes up to around 65,000 feet. A Russian firm, Beriev, is currently building three A-50 AWACS (Airborne Warning and Control Systems). Called the A-50Ehl, the surveillance aircraft will be the first of its kind to be built in Russia, which combines a variety of systems from Israel, India and Russia. The aircraft will be the Ilyushin IL-76TD transport aircraft with a PS-90A engine, and fitted with communications systems from Israel Aircraft Industry and surveillance software developed by Indian programmers and communications systems. The three aircraft are due to be delivered to India in 2005. It is pertinent to mention that Russia had offered its version of A-50 AWACS in April 2000, but after its thorough testing at the Chandigarh base in India, the offer was turned down.[32]

AWACS are regarded as 'eyes in the sky', which can see the airspace and also observe movements on the ground and the sea. The possession of AWACS offers unparalleled combat advantages. By observing enemy activities in advance, AWACS can position fighter jets in the air much before enemy planes arrive at a striking distance. The A-50 AWACS can search the sky up to a radius of 230km, and on its radar can pick up the ships around 400km away. Its liaison with the ground command post is around 350km away, but can be enhanced to 2000km.[33]

Indian Navy

At present, the Indian Navy (IN) possesses 16 operational submarines, and 26 principal surface combatants, with eight Destroyers and 12 frigates. The Indian Navy is demanding at least another 25 destroyers and frigates to guard the country's 7,516 km long coastline. India's sudden naval build-up can be understood from the fact that Indian Navy had played a prominent role in drafting India's nuclear doctrine and hence specific attention is being paid to the naval component of this doctrine. Moreover, *Hindustan Times* reported that the Indian Naval formal doctrine, expected to be unveiled shortly by the Chief of Naval Staff, former Admiral Sushil Kumar, is to chart a new course for the Navy – the force plans to be able to influence war on land. The new doctrine lists three areas of priority for the Navy; naval diplomacy; the building of a force with concentrated firepower but with the ability to react to contingencies rapidly; and the acquisition of land attack capability. The commissioning of the *INS Sindhushastra* (India's first missile-firing submarine) at Saint Petersburg on July 19, 2000 is thus part of a bigger design that sees the Navy taking part in conflicts off the coasts of other nations—a shift in policy from patrolling in coastal or brown waters to venturing in blue waters.[34]

This fact is further underscored by a Russian report, which says that India is expected to accomplish a large warship-building programme and set up a national nuclear submarine fleet. New Delhi plans to have five nuclear submarines capable of carrying missiles with nuclear warheads. It was further stated that these submarines would be equipped with Sagarika nuclear-capable missiles.[35]

To accomplish its objectives, India will take delivery of three Krivak Class frigates to be equipped with anti-ship and anti-submarine weapons to the Indian Navy by 2003. India has recently bought two Kilo Class submarines and three frigates from Russia. India and Russia also signed a protocol in October 2000, during the Russian President, Vladimir Putin's visit to India, regarding the purchase and refiting of the Admiral Gorshkov aircraft carrier, as well as some 40 MiG-29K aircraft for use on the Gorshkov. Moreover, Moscow based reports have also suggested that India is seeking Russian assistance in developing the nuclear reactor for an indigenously designed, nuclear submarine.[36] Moreover, India has begun to take deliveries of the first of a family of advanced Russian 3M-54E anti-ship and submarine-launched cruise missiles. Russia also supplied Brahmos, a new supersonic missile, which can be launched from ships and aircraft and can carry a nuclear warhead, and is virtually impossible to be shot down. Moreover, these missiles are likely to be fit on the advanced frigates being built at Bombay, and will 'substantially influence war on land'.[37]

India is also holding negotiations with Moscow for purchase of design and license to build Amur Class submarines. Besides, Russia is also constructing three Krivak class frigates, which will be armed with Klub missiles, which has features that qualify it to be a cruise missile. The Klub missile has two variants – the anti-ship and the land attack – and has a strike range of 300 kms. Moreover, Russia sold upgraded Type 53 (TEST-71) torpedoes to India, which can be used against either submarines or surface ships, and has a range of 20 kms. Besides, an advanced anti-submarine 90R missiles would also be delivered by Russia to India, which would effectively boost warfare capabilities of Indian navy. *The Times of India* also reported that, India is undergoing negotiations for the lease of a Charlie-1 class type of nuclear submarines. Besides, Russia is also manufacturing Talwar frigates for the Indian Navy, which will also be equipped with Klub anti-ship missiles. India and Russia have also finalised a three-year lease for a Russian Shuka-B Class nuclear-powered submarine for which india will pay US $ 25 million per year. The submarine was expected to reach India by January 2002.[38]

Apart from that, Russia will also deliver the first 5 Ka-31 helicopters to the Indian Navy in 2001-2002, which will be used for obtaining air navigation data, information on land approach and obstacles, display other flying vehicles, and patrolling of sea and coastal water area.[39] Besides, in October 2001, both India and Russia concluded talks for leasing four nuclear-capable TU-22 aircraft. Moreover, Indian Navy's TU-142 long-range reconnaissance aircraft and 5 IL-38 medium-range reconnaissance aircraft were sent back to Russia.

New Areas of Defense Cooperation between India and Russia

The two countries have signed several new agreements that will sustain cooperation through the coming years.

Admiral Gorshkov (INS Vikramaditya) Deal

The $1.5 billion deal for the purchase of the 45,000 tonne aircraft carrier *Admiral Gorshkov* was signed on January 20, 2004 after over a decade of negotiations. *Admiral Gorshkov* is an old Soviet ship and about 70 per cent of the carrier will be retrofitted. It is expected to arrive in India by the end of 2008. The wisdom of buying an 'old Soviet hull' has been disputed by several experts.[40] However, the Indian Navy greatly needed the aircraft carrier.

The Gorshkov deal was reportedly a part of the package that included the lease of two 971 Shchuka-B or Akula class nuclear submarines and several strategic Tu-22 (NATO designation 'Backfire') bombers. Subsequently, Russia was reported to have backed out of the nuclear submarine deal so as not to displease the Americans. The issue was in the news again. Citing Russian sources, Vladimir Radyuhin wrote in *The Hindu* (December 7, 2005) that the lease of nuclear-propelled submarines to India is in the pipeline. Under a $1.8-billion contract for a ten-year lease, the Russian side has resumed the construction of the subs, which was frozen in the 1990s. In October 2005, 200 Indian naval officers have started training at a submarine training centre at Sosnovij Bor near St. Petersburg.[41] Earlier, the Soviet Union had leased a nuclear-propelled submarine nicknamed *Chakra* to India from 1988 to 1991. The Navy is hopeful that the nuclear submarine will finally arrive.

India has issued a global tender for the purchase of 126 multi-role fighter aircraft. The deal is worth $5-6 billion. Contenders are American F- 16 Falcon and F/A-18 Super Hornet, the Swedish JAS-39 Gripen, the French Mirage-2000-5 and the Russian MiG-29M2. Russia will have to contend with other competitors. Rosoboron Service India Chairman Anatoly Negreev candidly remarked, "Russia is worried about losing out to US, France and Israel. We need to be more competitive....India is our destiny."[42]

BrahMos

The *BrahMos* supersonic cruise missile with the range of 280 km is based on 3M-55 Onyx missile designed by Russia's NPO Mashinostroyenia.[43] It is repeatedly cited as the shining example of joint research, development and production by India and Russia. The Indian Navy has already inducted the sea version of the missile. The land and air versions of the missile are in the process of development and likely induction. The Russian military so far has not inducted it. Russia needs to change its laws before its induction, which it has promised to do. The two countries also decided to jointly market *BrahMos* to third countries by 2007, by which time India and Russia we expected to finalise sale procedures and put into space at least 18 satellites under GLONASS to track the missile's movements. *BrahMos* is just one example of joint collaboration. The IPR agreement cleared the deck for more such projects. In view of difficulties and snags in the development of indigenous technologies, such collaboration might be the best way for India to acquire and develop new technologies.

Vth Generation Fighter Aircraft

For several years, the two sides have been considering joint development of the 5th generation multi-role fighter aircraft and transport aircraft. The intention was reiterated during the December 2005 visit of the Indian Prime Minister. The Russian government has already selected the Sukhoi aviation firm for the purpose and likewise allocated funds.

However, the size of the Sukhoi aircraft does not find favour with Indians.[48]*RIA Novosti* (January 18, 2006) in one of its news report has argued that Moscow should develop both a light-engine plane and a heavy fighter. Russia needs a heavy-duty fighter as its "weaponry and electronics have always been bulky."[44] The Sukhoi-developed 5th generation fighter would be a heavy aircraft. Further, India and France might help Russia to develop a light-engine warplane, which could become popular in the international market. A competition is going on between the Sukhoi and MiG aviation firms in Russia. MiG proposes to build a lighter aircraft.

Medium Transport Aircraft Development Programme (MTA)

The development of MTA has been assigned greater urgency in India. MTA negotiations began in the late 1990s and in 2000 the $700-million project became part of the 10-year Indian-Russian military-technical cooperation programme. The investment was shared between Russian aircraft maker Irkut and India's HAL (Hindustan Aeronautics Ltd). Subsequently, differences between the two came to light as the Russians wanted 19.5 tonnes of carrying capacity while the Indians are satisfied with 14-16 tonnes.[45]

Russia wants to develop PS-12 engine to power the aircraft at the cost of $3-4 billion. The Indians are inclined to use French or US engines. Recent reports suggest the sides are close to agreement to resolve the issue. The cargo carrying capacity of the MTA will be 20 tonnes, but the Indian MTAs will be powered by Snecma Moteurs' CFM 56-7 Turbofans. Solutions for the glass cockpits will be considered from the French firm Thales. IAF will acquire 45 and the Russian side 60 units.[46]

Cooperation in Space – the GLONASS

During President Putin's visit to India in December 2004, an agreement was signed between Roskosmos and ISRO on the joint use of the Sovietera Global Navigational Satellite System (GLONASS) by making it fully functional by joint efforts, including the launching of new Russian satellites from Indian launch pads with the help of Indian vehicles. The deal will reduce India's dependence on the US GPS (Global Positioning System), which may be denied in times of conflict. During Prime Minister Manmohan Singh's December 2005 Moscow visit, an agreement was signed on measures to protect technology during long-term co-operation in joint development, operation and use of the GLONASS for peaceful purposes.[53] Vladimir Radyuhin, however, opines that GLONASS shall be used by both the countries for civil as well as military purposes.[47]

Joint Military Exercises

During past few years, Indo-US military-to-military cooperation has greatly expanded. In contrast, Indo-Russian defence cooperation has largely been in the military-technical field. Recently, Russia also has shown greater interest in boosting military-to-military ties. In October 2005, the two armies and navies held joint exercises in the desert of Rajasthan and off the coast of Vishakhapatnam, respectively.

Problems and Weaknesses in the Indo-Russian Defence Relations

Machinery and equipment in the Russian defence industries are becoming old and out-dated. It has been pointed out that during 1999 and 2000, less than 5 per cent of the machinery was less than five years old, while over 75 per cent were more than 10 years old. About one-third of the machinery was more than 20 years old. Ageing manpower is another problem. The average age of the workers is mid-fifties. Younger people are not attracted to defence industry jobs. There is in general a shortage of funds for R&D. The dependence on exports is yet another limitation. Moreover, the Russian defence industrial sector is known for its general lack of transparency.[48] It appears unlikely that the Soviet mentality will change overnight. All this is cautioning Indian policymakers not to risk putting all eggs in one basket and diversify the source of defence supplies.

Most of the weapon systems that permitted Russia to emerge as one of the two biggest arms exporters were essentially developed by the Soviet Union in 1970s and 1980s. These weapons successfully competed with their foreign equivalents. Russian experts apprehend that India and China have purchased most of what Russia can offer. The two may look to other sources for more advanced weapon systems and technology, and arms exports to India and China may, in fact, decline after 2007-2008. It is imperative for Russia to develop new weapon systems to remain a major arms exporter. While there are instances of Russia developing new weapons and upgrading existing ones, the US Army on its part has embarked on an ambitious multi-billion dollar Future Combat Systems (FCS) programme.

Problem of Spare Parts

The easy availability of cheap spare parts is a problem area in any defence relationship. The problem existed even during the Soviet period. There were delays and bottlenecks in getting timely supply of spare parts. While the Soviet weapons were cheap, Soviet spare parts were not. Thus a retired Lt. General of the Indian Army has stressed that although the import of Soviet weapon systems has been of immense benefit, there have been persistent problems of maintenance and support. Interestingly, the blame is not put squarely on the Soviet Union/Russia alone. It appears that the Indian side did not pay adequate attention to details while concluding initial agreements in which clauses for product support were not included. Once the weapons were acquired, India was at the mercy of the supplier for spare parts.

There was lack of openness on the part of the Soviet side and also lack of communication and understanding of each other's systems. Due to the climatic conditions in India, there is a greater wear and tear of equipment. Also, those who actually used the equipment were not involved in negotiations. Owing to the "antiquated system of inventory control and maintenance in Indian Ordinance Depots," spares received at times disappeared and were not easy to locate when needed thereby adding to the stories of poor Russian response to India's demands for spares. The problem of spares and maintenance was further aggravated as some of the equipment was getting obsolete in its country of origin by the time it was acquired in the late 1960s and early 1970s.[49]

In 2000, the state arms monopoly *Rosoboronexport* was created. It controls 90 per cent of Russian arms exports and also seeks to establish monopoly on the supply of spare parts. According to Victor Komardin military spare parts bought by India from unauthorised dealers were to blame for non-optimal performance and other problems in Russian-built equipment. He admitted that spares bought from his company would be more expensive as well as require time to deliver.[50] In fact, the price quoted by Rosoboronexport is several times higher. In 2001, the then Vice Admiral Arun Prakash reportedly 'blasted' the Russian arms dealers for lack of transparency regarding pricing and low quality of spares. He said that it was difficult to ascertain whether the delivered parts were new or old. He emphasised the need for Russia to streamline the arms trade and clarify the prices of equipment. The Indian side resents Rosoboronexport's efforts to have a monopoly on the supply of spare parts when identical hardware is available in the market at significantly lower prices. Indeed, in all the meetings of the intergovernmental commission on military-technical cooperation, India has been persistently taking up the issue of product support for equipment of Soviet/ Russian origin.[51]

Impact of Growing Competition for Indian Arms Market

As Russia is facingh increasing competition in the Indian arms market, it is showing greater willingness to respond to Indian needs. The recent setting up of a consignment warehouse and a service centre in India called Rosoboron Service may go a long way in meeting India's requirements for timely and uninterrupted supply of spare parts and repair and maintenance of equipment of Soviet and Russian origin. It is a joint venture involving eight Russian defence manufacturers and an Indian company comprising ex-servicemen called *Krasny Mir*. Initially, the Rosoboron Service will meet the needs of the Indian Navy. Subsequently, it will also cater to the requirements of the Indian Air Force. For the IAF, Rosoboron Service will set up a new MRO (Maintenance, Repair, and Overhaul) centre in Nasik for MiG29B-12 and Su-30MKIs. A number of Russian companies plan to set up 'bonded spares warehouses and dedicated workshops' for undertaking MRO activities for the Indian Air force.[52]

Of late, reports have appeared that in view of persistent complaints, the Russian government is also willing to partially reduce Rosoboronexport's monopoly. The Russian government is willing to allow 20 top Russian defence firms to sign international spare parts and upgrade contracts on their own, bypassing Rosoboronexport.

No More 'Friendship' Prices

If the main motive behind the Soviet arms transfers was geo-political, the main motive behind Russian arms transfers is commercial. A retired Vice Admiral said the following regarding the situation immediately after the collapse of the Soviet Union: Russia adopted free market philosophy. They started demanding unreasonably high prices for their hardware. They started making unreasonable demands. Russian price demande became equal to the Western, but they did not provide detailed break-up of costing and Russian technology also lacked the sophistication of the Western countries.[53]

No wonder, Russia is not prepared to supply weapons to India on prices and terms offered by the former Soviet Union. In April 2001, an Indian parliamentary report noted that Russia no longer grants India 'friendship prices'.[54] The report recommended that India should opt for global bids for all its defence procurements.[55] In the initial post-Soviet period, India wanted rupee payment, but Russia insisted on hard currency payments. Now, in any case, the rupee payment regime has come to an end and all transactions have shifted to hard currency.

Delay in Supply

Delay in the supply of equipment has been a constant problem. For instance, the deadlines set for the supply of Su-30 MKI were not met. There were also delays in the upgradation of MiG-21 to the MiG-21-93 level.[56] It has been reported that the Su-30 MKI aircraft that India has been receiving did not have all the features. Of the 32 aircraft received from Russia, 22 were phase I and phase II variants. There were only 10 phase III fighters but even they did not have some critical components such as electronic warfare system, reconnaissance pod and high accuracy direction finder radar warning receiver. However, the Russians have agreed to incorporate these systems into all aircraft at their cost.[57]

India has asked Russia to conclude an MoU for providing bank guarantees on timely supply of weapon systems and spares. In place of the bank guarantee, the Finance Ministry of Russia has given a "comfort letter" for ensuring adherence to the delivery schedule and New Delhi can 'encash' it in lieu of penalty.[58]

Concern about Quality

At times, there have been complaints of substandard systems and spare parts. At times, the contractual obligations are not met. It was reported that in case of Tangushka Air Defence system, old and rusted systems were provided. However, when the Indian Army drew the attention to this, they were replaced.[59] To cite yet another example, reports suggested a number of lacunae in the latest T-90 tanks supplied to India. The strength of T-90 tanks lies in their missile firing capability, which even the French, German or the US tanks do not have. However, the T-90s supplied to India were without the missile firing system. The manufacturers subsequently promised to equip the tanks with missiles. The engines of the T-90 tanks also have the persisting problem of overheating.[60]

Upgrading and Modernisation

It is widely felt that Russia has not been successful in developing the advanced subsystems that make up the bulk of modernisation activities. Such activities are expected to grow in co-operation with foreign companies.[61] In fact, Israeli companies have become very active in the modernisation of Soviet/Russian military equipment to some consternation of the Russians. Naturally, the Russians are wary of Israeli competition. None the less, the two reached a compromise by signing in March 2003 an Intellectual Property Rights agreement, whereby Israel undertook to involve Russian companies in modernisation of Russian equipment.[62]

The issue of Indian Navy's Tu-142 aircraft upgrade plan is particularlyillustrative. In August 2004, India originally turned to Russia for upgrade, but balked at the $888-million price tag put by Rosoboronexport. Then India approached Israel Aircraft Industries to upgrade the aircraft with multi-mission avionics and electronic warfare systems. Russia's consent was mandatory, but Moscow was reluctant. Moscow also reportedly insisted that its Sea Dragon Electronic warfare systems be part of the upgrade plans. Finally, the Indian Navy advised the government to scrap the plan for upgrade and to launch a global tender to replace all the eight aircraft.[63]

Amidst numerous complaints about the delays in the supply of weapons and spare parts and at times their poor quality, the Soviet/Russian weapons have proved to be battle-worthy and reliable. In fact, during Indo- US joint air exercises in Gwalior in February 2004, the Indian pilots flying Mig-21 Bisons, MiG-27, MiG-29s Su-30s out-performed the US pilots by their training and skills. The success of Indian pilots flying Russian fighter aircraft was hailed with pride across Russia and the other former Soviet republics.

Signing of Intellectual Property Rights (IPR) Agreement

The bane of the Indian defence establishment is the failure to develop indigenous weapon systems of the requisite quality within the planned time. Russian equipment was purchased in bulk as a stopgap arrangement in the hope that it will be replaced by indigenous MBTs and LCAs. This did not materialise and a dependency has been created on imported hardware.

For the past couple of years, Russia had been insisting that India sign the IPR agreement regarding defence cooperation. The agreement was finally signed during Prime Minister Manmohan Singh's visit to Moscow in December 2005. Apprehensive of India diversifying defence equipment sources, Russia was keen to safeguard its financial and intellectual property rights. The IPR issue became a sore point. Russian Defence Minister Sergei Ivanov warned, "We will find it difficult to move forward in high-end defence technologies without an agreement on the protection of intellectual property. We will not hand over technologies for nothing. Russia is not Soviet Union."[64] Russia also put pressure on New Delhi. India was warned that the doors of Russian defence factories would be shut to Indian military and technicians in the absence of an IPR agreement.[65] In November 2005, Russia refused to transfer technology as part of its planned sale of Igla surface-to-air missile systems. Earlier, in late September 2005, Russia said it would not give the technology along with the Smerch Multibarrel Rocket Launcher system and reduced the order from 69 pieces to 46.[66]

Russia has conceded the Indian demand that the IPR provisions apply to future transactions only. The accord is intended to ensure that no technology is transferred to third countries and royalty is paid to Russia for work performed on Russian-built weapons by other countries. Reports suggest that the terms of IPR agreement also mention Russia as India's preferred supplier. Some Indian defence experts have cautioned against such a provision. However, India reportedly agreed to the clause as it is still "too dependent on Russian arms supplies."[67]

Conclusion

The competition for a share of the Indian arms market is growing among major suppliers. The post-Pokhran sanctions on India by the US were removed in November 2001. Israel has emerged as the second biggest arms exporter to India after Russia. Diversification ensures that a country can not be held to ransom by a sole supplier. It can also lead to lower prices as well as access to various technologies. However, diverse suppliers cause the problem of interoperability of different types of equipment, while a single source of supply leads to standardisation of equipment. On their part, the Indian armed forces have the experience of using and integrating different types of equipment.

Moscow had previously balked at India's attempts to diversify arms supply, especially when India opted for the British Hawk AJT (Advanced Jet Trainer) instead of MiG-AT.[68] But, Russia appears to have finally reconciled to the inevitable change. A PTI dispatch from Moscow on January 18, 2004, quoted the Russian Defence Minister Sergei Ivanov as saying: "We had never planned to monopolise the Indian (arms) market. Depending only on one source is bad for any armed forces, it leads to their degradation."[69] Ivanov said that Russia understands India's desire to get the best available technology and welcomes it, and has to compete by offering the best technology. Referring to the Israeli Phalcon Radar Deal that would be fitted into Il-78 tanker aircraft, he added that Moscow was not averse to ties with third parties while working on Indian defence orders. He also referred to the French and Israeli systems having been incorporated in Su-30 MKI multi-role fighter aircraft designed and developed for India. The Russian defence industry itself is changing, for instance, Russian NPO Saturn and French Snecma have set up a joint venture called Power Jet that produces SaM 146 aircraft engines. The engine is believed to "represent all the latest know-how."[70] The European

Aerospace and Defence System (EADS) has purchased a 10 per cent stake in Russia's Irkut aviation company.[71]

Owing to past legacy and long-term dependence, Russia is likely to remain a major defence partner. In a keynote address to the General Staff Academy of the Russian Armed Forces, the Indian Defence Minister, George Fernandes, said that Russia "has been, and remains the largest source of our arms, weapon systems and technology imports."[72] He emphasised that the recent strengthening of defence ties with many countries "is not at the expense of our traditional friendly relations with Russia which remain unique, time-tested and steadfast."[73] Even if no new weapons are purchased, India will continue to need spare parts for the weaponry of Soviet/Russian origin and also depend on Russia for their upgrades and modernisation. The licence production of 140 Su-30 MKI under a $3.5 billion deal, itself will go on till 2017-2018.

While diversifying arms acquisitions, India would not like to risk the derailment of the current system that may pose potential security hazards in the near term. India would like to maintain its strategic autonomy and decide each issue on the basis of merit and from the standpoint of India's national interests. Steps have been taken of late to streamline defence acquisition procedure and make it more transparent, speedy and accountable.[74]

Cooperation with Soviet Union and now Russia has made a vitally important contribution to the development of Indian defence potential. It has given India access to sophisticated weapons and advanced technologies at a time when others were not willing. The defence cooperation reflected the convergence of their larger geopolitical interests. In the post-Soviet difficult transition period, arms purchases by India and China have helped the Russian MIC to tide over the crisis and survive. As a major arms supplier to both India and China, Russia has been persistently pressing for 'triangular'[75] cooperation among Russia, China and India. However, despite the recent improvement in India's relations with China, in view of the disputed status of the Sino-Indian border and other security concerns, India cannot afford to lower its guard. Russian arms supply to China and the possibility of further transfer of Russian arms and technology to Pakistan through China, do add to New Delhi's worries. At the same time, if India distances itself, it may make Russia even more dependent on China.

No country can be fully self-reliant in all areas of defence-related technology. Moreover, today's trend is towards joint development and production of defence equipment. According to the emerging opinion in the Indian strategic community, the country must be self-reliant in areas where technology denial regimes are imposed, like nuclear and missile technologies. India may concentrate on developing and further expanding the areas of her core competence. In other areas, the country may opt for overseas partners, including Russia. Joint development and production of new weapon systems may emerge as a very promising area of continued Indo-Russian cooperation. It may provide continuity and stability to existing ties. Advanced avionics and electronic systems developed by Western countries and Israel may also be incorporated as is already being done.

Competition among the suppliers may indeed be good and has already produced beneficial results. There is a need to handle the emerging situation with dexterity and savoir by giving attention to details and nuances. In the pursuit of its enlightened national interests, it is to be expected that India would seek to leverage its position as a major defence buyer, and so would Russia as a supplier. In the twenty-first century geopolitical scenario, all the major actors are engaging each other. None the less, India's ties with Russia will continue to be driven by not only common strategic and geopolitical interests but also shared interest in the defence sector. They would, however, need to adjust policies wherever necessary for enhancing mutual gains in this vital sector if they want to sustain a robust relationship in the new global environment.

References

1. Verinder Grover, *International Relations and Foreign Policy of India*, Vol. 7, Deep & Deep Publications, Rajouri Garden, New Delhi, 1992, p.124.
2. Ibid., p.426.
3. Ibid., p.496.
4. Dr Subhash Kapila, 'India-Russia Strategic Cooperation: Time to move away?', *Strategic Affairs*, www.stratmag.com/ issueOct-1/ page 06.htm

5. Verinder Grover, op.cit., p.163.
6. K. Arif, Pakistan's Foreign Policy, *Indian Perspective,* Vanguard Books Ltd, Lahore, 1984, pp. 282-283.
7. Verinder Grover, op.cit., p. 161.
8. Anita Inder Singh, 'India's Relations with Russia and Central Asia', *International Affairs,* RIIA, Vol. 71, No. 1, 1995.
9. Jerome M. Conley, 'Indo-Russian Military And Nuclear Cooperation: Implications for US Security Interests', USAF Institute for National Security Studies, www.fas.org/nuke/guide/india/ doctrine/ocp32.htm
10. Dr Subhash Kapila, op.cit.
11. Jerome M. Conley, op.cit.
12. 'Indo-Russian joint declaration', *The News,* October 4, 2000.
13. Jerome M. Conley, op.cit.
14. 'India forms defence council to speed acquisition process', *Defence News,* August 31, 2001, www.bharat-rakshak.com
15. 'India to buy 320 Russian T-90 tanks', *Indian Express,* April 3, 2000.
16. 'India inks deal for 310 Russian T-90 tanks', www.bharat-rakshak.com
17. 'India nears massive network upgrades', *Defence News,* September 21, 2001
18. 'Russia to supply improved Bofors shells, April 12, 2000, www.bharat-rakshak.com
19. 'IAF wants 20 squadrons within 20 years', *Defence News,* October 23, 2000.
20. 'India stretches life span of aircraft', *Defence News,* July 10, 2000.
21. 'More on India's MiG-21 upgrade', *Jane's Defence Upgrades,* March 16, 2001.
22. 'SU-30s to be made in India this year', *Indian Express,* June 10, 2000.
23. 'Indian version of Sukhoi world's best', *Times of India,* August 2, 2001.
24. India, Russia sign Sukhoi Su-30 MKI deal, *Times of India,* December 28, 2001.
25. 'India, Russia to discuss LCA production', February 27, 2001, www.bharat-rakshak.com
26. 'Russia may open service centre for its fighter aircraft supplied to India', *Indian Express,* February 28, 2001.
27. 'New air defences for India will unnerve Beijing', June 21, 2001, www.bharat-rakshak.com

28. HAL plans to raise $650 million for 100-seater aircraft, February 9, 2001, www.bharat-rakshak.com
29. 'India offered 'Mystic-B aircraft, *Jane's Defence Weekly,* July 6, 2001.
30. 'India developing new surveillance software', August 6, 2001, www.bharat-rakshak.com
31. 'Navy all set to chart new course', *Hindustan Times,* July 20, 2001.
32. 'India Navy's sub sail from Russia', *Times of India,* August 25, 2001.
33. 'India begins to receive Russian missiles for subs', *Defence News,* October 23, 2001.
34. 'India reworks Russian missile to make it N-capable', *The Statesman,* October 22, 2001.
35. 'Indian submarines to have missiles soon'; October 6, 2001, www.bharat-rakshak.com
36. 'Torpedo upgrades from Russia', *Janes Defence Upgrade,* November 1, 2001.
37. 'India to hire Russian N-sub again', *Times of India,* December 20, 2000.
38. 'India settles nuclear sub lease terms with Russia', *Defecse News,* October 15, 2001.
39. 'One Ka-31 to be delivered before 2001', *Itar-Tass,* March 29, 2001.
40. *Hindustan Times,* December 8, 2005.
41. Rahul Bedi, "India and Russia Strengthen Defence Ties", *Jane's Defence Weekly,* December 14, 2005, p. 8.
42. *The Indian Express,* October 7, 2005.
43. *Strategic Digest,* November 2005, P- 1509, from *Aviation Week & Space Technology,* September 2005.
44. Biplob Gogoi, "Military-Technical collaboration between India and Russia: An Overview of the Post-Soviet Period", *India Quarterly,* 58 (3-4), July-December 466 *Strategic Analysis/Apr-Jun 2006,* 2002, p.307.
45. *Jane's Defence Weekly,* December 14, 2005, p.16.
46. *Strategic Digest,* September 2004, from *Flight International,* August 3-9, 2004, pp.1289-90.
47. *SIPRI Yearbook, 2005,* pp. 419, 422.
48. *Strategic Digest,* August 2005 from *Biznes,* July 19, 2005, pp.1078-79.
49. "India and Russia set to boost space cooperation", at www.indiainfo.com, May13, 2005; Also, *Strategic Digest,* June, 2005 from *RIA Novosti,* May 2005.
50. www.kremlin.ru, December 6, 2005.

51. *The Hindu,* December 7, 2005.
52. R.G. Gidadhubli, "Russia Refurbishing the Military-Industrial Complex", *Economic and Political Weekly,* August 23, 2003, p.3546.
53. *Vedomosti,* June 16, 2005 in *Strategic Digest,* July 2005, pp. 895-96.
54. Robert Hewson, "Russia's PGMs Go on Show", *Jane's Defence Weekly,* October 19, 2005, p. 6; Robert Hewson, "Russia Launches R-73 Upgrade", *Jane's Defence Weekly,* August 24, 2005, p. 5.
55. *Jane's Defence Weekly,* August 24, 2005, p. 25.
56. V.K. Singh, "Indo-Russian Defence Co-operation and Self-Reliance: An Army View Point", *Agni,* 7 (1), May-August 2003, PP- 5-7.
57. *The Tribune,* November 30, 2002.
58. "Indian Admiral Blasts Russian Arms Deals", at http://www.aeronautics.ru /archive/aeronews/conv/article_April_2001 _ 10_118.htm. *India-Russia Defence Co-operation* 465.
59. Prasun K. Sengupta, "Soaring Cooperation", *Force,* 3 (6), February 2006, pp. 36-37.
60. *Gazeta,* September 8, 2005, in *Strategic Digest,* October 2005, p.1380.
61. R.B. Suri, "Indo-Russian Co-operation in the Naval Field and Self-Reliance", *Agni,* 7 (1), May-August 2003, pp. 22-23.
62. V. Raghuvanshi, "Report urges India to widen contracting process", *Defense News,* April 30, 2001, p. 6; *SIPRI Yearbook 2002,* p. 378.
63. *SIPRI Yearbook 2000,* p.352.
64. *The Hindu,* September 5, 2005.
65. *The Hindu,* November 16, 2005.
66. "From Strength to Strength: Growing Military Co-operation", *Force,* January 2005, p.18.
67. "Still lumbering, the hurriedly concluded T-90s tank deal is bearing fruits now", Ibid., p. 19.
68. *SIPRI Yearbook 2003,* p. 444.
69. *SIPRI Yearbook 2004,* p.456.
70. *Strategic Digest,* October 2004 from *Defence News,* August 30, 2004, pp.1433-34.
71. Chidanand Rajghatta, "Ageing IAF shoots down USAF top guns", *Times of India,* June 18, 2004.
72. Vivek Raghuvanshi, "Russia Denies Missile Technology to India", *Defence News,* November 28, 2005. Following the signing of the IPR agreement, it was reported that the Indian Army will produce six

batteries of Smerch-M multi-barrel rocket launchers, their 9M528 rockets worth $ 450 million.

73. *Strategic Digest*, July 2005 from *Defence News*, May 9, 2005, pp.894-95.
74. "India Looks to US for Weapons after Delay in Russian Deals", at http://www.rense.com/general19/IndialooksAL.htm.
75. *India's Defence Procurement Procedure*, June 2005.

5

India and Russia as Strategic Partners in Post-Cold War Period (1991-2003)

Introduction

Indo-Russian relations are civilisational and time-tested. These have traditionally been based on continuity, trust and mutual understanding. The importance attached to them cuts across party lines in India and is not subject to political vicissitudes. There is a national consensus on the need for a strong and stable relationship with the Russian Federation. A similar consensus exists in Russia on close and friendly ties with India. The 100th anniversary of the opening of the Russian Consulate General in Mumbai was commemorated on November 22, 2000. After the disintegration of the USSR and the emergence of Russia as an independent State, Russia declared itself to be "State-continuator"[1] of the erstwhile USSR. India recognised Russia as the successor-State to the former Soviet Union. India's relations with the Russian Federation are multifaceted and encompass different sectors including political consultations, economic and commercial relations and cooperation in trade and economy, science and technology, culture, education and defence. It is significant that India and Russia are the world's largest democracies, India in terms of the size of the population and Russia in terms of its size.

In the new Foreign Policy Concept released by Russian Federation on July 10, 2000, it has been stated that one of the crucial directions in the Russian foreign policy in Asia will be to develop friendly relations with the leading Asian states including India. It further states that Russia intends to strengthen its traditional partnership with India, including in international affairs.

Indo-Russian Relations during the Post-Cold War Period

India and Russia have enjoyed close strategic relations during much of the cold war era. The relations were all-encompassing, and were the result of the geostrategic and geopolitical alignments that dominated much of the cold war era. While India's arch rival, Pakistan, established closer relations with the US and the West, India fell into the lap of the former Soviet Union (FSU). Throughout the cold war, the FSU provided India with the crucial political, economic, military and moral support needed to put the latter on the way to economic prosperity and political and military strength. However, the military cooperation remained the most prominent aspect of their bilateral relations, with the FSU accounting for nearly 75 per cent of the military hardware possessed by India till the disintegration of the former in December 1991.[2] Both countries signed the Treaty of Peace, Friendship and Cooperation in August 1971, in which the dominant aspect was the emphasis on security clauses. As a consequence, India benefited from the FSU's support to its covert, and later overt role in the creation of Bangladesh in 1971. On its part, India remained supportive of FSU's policies throughout the cold war era, especially the Soviet invasion of Afghanistan in 1979.[3]

In the post-cold war era, the Russian Federation, the successor of the FSU, in a much weakened position having lost the status of a superpower, had to reorient its foreign policy in the context of its own altered status and the developing geo-strategic environment. During this period of transition, under Russia's first Foreign Minister, Andrei Kozyrev (1992-1995), the overall orientation of the Russian foreign policy was a 'Look West'[4] policy that was Eurocentric, and establishing good relations with the US was its top priority. Thus, during that period, Asia in general, and South Asia in particular, was accorded a low priority in Moscow's restructuring process. In January 1993, the Russian Foreign Ministry published the *Concept of Russian Federation's Foreign Policy,* in which South Asia was accorded seventh place in its list of ten priorities.[5]

India, on its part, also felt the need to diversify its relations from that of dependence on Russia to establishing more fruitful relations with the US, Western Europe, Japan and South East Asian countries. In both cases, the restructuring phase was also subject to a host of domestic political developments, which exerted their respective influence on foreign relations. Nevertheless, the earlier formal diplomatic contact was maintained through these transitional years. Although, the Russian former President, Boris Yeltsin, paid an official visit to India in January 1993, and both countries renewed the Treaty of Friendship and Cooperation, which was an extension of the previous Treaty of Peace Friendship and Cooperation of 1971, the significant aspect was that the security clauses present in the treaty of 1971 were dropped. While their bilateral relations received an impetus, yet much needed to be done to revive the old warmth in their relations.[6]

The then Indian Prime Minister, Narasimha Rao, reciprocated Yeltsin's visit in July 1994. Both leaders signed the Moscow Declaration on the Further Development and Intensification of Cooperation, and the Moscow Declaration on the Protection of the Interests of Pluralistic States, assuring international and bilateral goodwill and continuation of Russian arms and military equipment exports to India. Moreover, bilateral relations between India and Russia improved as a result of eight agreements signed in December 1994 during the visit of Russian Prime Minister, Viktor Chernomyrdin, to India. The agreements covered military and technical cooperation from 1995 to 2000; merchant shipping; promotion and mutual protection of investments; and trade and outer space cooperation. In March 1995, both countries signed agreements aimed at suppressing illegal weapons smuggling and drug trafficking. The visits of 1993 and 1994, followed by the appointment of Yevgeny Primakov as the Foreign Minister in January 1996, rekindled the desire on the part of the two countries to work out a strategic partnership. In March 1997, the Indian Prime Minister paid a visit to Russia which was followed by Russian Prime Minister, Primakov's visit to India in December 1998.[7] The following reasons could be ascribed in this search for deepening the relations of the two countries.

Firstly, Russia's initial bonhomie with the West could not deliver the expected financial and political support the former needed to resuscitate its morbid Soviet-era economic and political institutions, and their subsequent conversion into thriving institutions of free-market economy and democracy. Levels of foreign aid and investment expected by Russia from the US and the West were far below Russian expectations, and were completely tied to the import of Western goods. Hence, as an observer commented, "while ideological proximity and alliance with the West was to be given emphasis (not necessarily priority), Russian foreign policy aims were to be realised in the CIS Near Abroad, and with old allies in West Asia and South Asia."

Secondly, ever since the establishment of an independent Russia, its interests in Europe, West Asia and in Asia have clashed with those of the US. A number of positions taken by Russia showed the areas of divergence. Russia was opposed to the inclusion of the newly independent countries of its former East European satellites in NATO. It opposed the US policy in the Balkans, especially the NATO bombing of Kosovo without the implicit or explicit authorisation of the UN. It continued to support the governments of Iran and then Saddam-led Iraq. And finally, the West's opposition to Russia's policy in Chechnya caused further frictions. To ward off the increasing US unilateralism in the international arena, Russia laid emphasis on multipolarity. Its 'Look East' policy to co-opt India and China in a 'strategic triangle' formed part of this new thrust. From India's point of view, Russia's Chechen problem with its common factor of a Muslim resistance enabled it to enmesh its own domestic Kashmir-related political problems within the Russian foreign policy under the formulation of linking the *intifada* in Kashmir and the Chechen proclamation of independence to a larger growing phenomenon of terrorism on the world stage.

Thirdly, Russia was conscious of the Central Asian Republics' vulnerability to the political influence being exerted by the Western Europe and Turkey on the one hand, and Pakistan, Iran and Saudi Arabia on the other. It was equally concerned about the US security plans in the Western Pacific, to deal with potential crisis related to Taiwan and mainland China's confrontationist territorial claims in Southeast Asia. China and India relations grew in importance, as factors to balance US strategic postures in the Western Pacific, in arms control and disarmament, and in the management of the security environment in Southeast Asia. Russia forged its own independent course by expanding its defence relations with China, and re-emphasising its relations with India.[8]

Still another reason was that Moscow's initial policy makers (1992-1995) were also anxious to present a new face of a refurbished, post-communist nation devoid of previous baggage, and the special relationship with India was seen as a legacy of the past. Moscow, therefore, pressed on with remodeling its foreign policy to adjust to changed circumstances. Russian Vice President, Alexander Rutskoi, proclaimed the objective of positive relations with Muslim states in South and Central Asia, including Pakistan, to be established with the idea of maintaining an 'equidistance' between New Delhi and Islamabad. Pakistan assumed importance for Russia, since its help was needed by the latter to avoid the destabilisation effects on Central Asia, being caused by the infighting among various Mujahideen groups vying for power in Afghanistan. Also, Russia desired to seek help from Pakistan regarding the Russian POWs still missing in Afghanistan after the withdrawal of the FSU from Afghanistan in 1989.[9]

Russia's initial foreign policy initiatives *vis-à-vis* the West did not result in the kind of fruitful political and economic relations that it hoped for. Hence, Russia sought to diversify its foreign relations by resuscitating strategic relations with its Soviet-era allies, like India. India's desire to maintain warm relations with Russia was driven by its military needs and political opportunism, like its desire for a permanent seat in the UNSC. A major breakthrough was achieved when the Russian President, Vladimir Putin, paid an official visit to India in October 2000. Both countries signed a 'Declaration on Strategic Partnership', and ten agreements covering various aspects of bilateral relations. The Declaration spelt out in detail the long-term nature of Indo-Russian relations in all aspects of mutual cooperation, like political, defence, economic and trade, science and technological, and cultural spheres. Also, the Joint Statement issued at the conclusion of the bilateral talks affirmed Indian and Russian positions on various bilateral, regional and international issues.

The Putin visit was reciprocated by that of the Indian Prime Minister, Atal Behari Vajpayee, to Russia in November 2001. In the second visit of President Putin to India in December 2002, both countries signed a 'Declaration on Further Consolidation of Strategic Partnership' between them. These visits have resulted in the signing of numerous agreements encompassing political, defence, economic, legal, and cultural aspects of their relations.

As an Indian analyst pointed out, the Strategic Partnership was all encompassing in that 'both countries included political, economic, cultural and scientific cooperation simultaneously with defence and geo-strategy as part of their understanding of a security partnership'. Furthermore, this new relationship "broadened the concept of security itself, and "balanced the earlier relations that gave a privileged position to defence-related security".[10]

In order to evaluate the nature as well as the strength of their relationship, it will be appropriate to consider these relations the various aspects of the cooperation they designate: political; trade and economics; scientific and technological; military-technical cooperation; cultural; and nuclear cooperation. Furthermore, the political cooperation between the two countries is further subdivided into: cooperation in the fight against terrorism; Chechnya and Kashmir; Afghanistan; Central Asia; multipolarity and strategic stability; inter-institutional cooperation; cooperation on multilateral foras, etc.

India and Russia as a Strategic Partner in Post-Cold War Period

A Declaration on Strategic Partnership between the Republic of India and the Russian Federation was signed during the State Visit of President Putin to India in October 2000. This is a document of cardinal significance and marks a new step forward in the elaboration of the principles of our bilateral relations. It lays down the broad contours of bilateral relations between India and the Russian Federation in the twenty-first century.

Political Cooperation

Political cooperation between India and Russia has emerged as the dominant framework in their bilateral relations. Following Putin's visit to India in October 2000, it led to an intensification of political cooperation in the shape of the holding of annual summits, and regular ministerial-level consultations that now form an intrinsic facet of their bilateral relations. Both countries have intensified their cooperation on various political issues that include: terrorism; uprising in Chechnya and Kashmir; evolving situation in Afghanistan; Central Asia; joint efforts for a multipolar world on bilateral as well as multilateral foras. Both countries hold unanimous views on regional and international issues, and coordinate their efforts on various foras. A brief overview of their cooperation on the issues mentioned above are given below.

Fight against terrorism

Both Russia and India are faced with separatist movements in their respective regions of Chechnya and Kashmir based on the right for self-determination. Both countries have failed to curb these freedom movements. Both countries project and equate these movements for self-determination with terrorism. Both they also believe that these movements have the backing of some regional countries, which are extending them moral, political and financial support. In the Joint Statement issued at the end of President Putin's visit to India in October 2000, the two sides underlined the importance of joint efforts in "combating international terrorism." Both believed that the Taliban-ruled Afghanistan had become a 'breeding ground' for sponsoring and promoting 'extremism' in Chechnya and Indian-held Kashmir. Both agreed to set up a Joint Working Group (JWG) on Afghanistan. From the Indian point of view it could be considered a gain in that during Putin's address to the Joint Session of the Indian Parliament during the same visit, he had said that the same extremist organisations that were creating problems in Jammu & Kashmir were behind the troubles in Chechnya and other northern territories of Russia.

To further institutionalise and consolidate their cooperation on terrorism, the two countries signed the 'Moscow Declaration on International Terrorism'[11] during Indian Prime Minister, A. B. Vajpayee's visit to Russia in November 2001. It states: 'In multi-ethnic and democratic countries, such as India and the Russian Federation, violent actions being perpetrated under the slogan of self-determination, in reality represents acts of terrorism, which in most cases have strong international links.'[6] Both sides also stressed the need for the early finalisation of the 'Convention for the Suppression of Acts of Nuclear Terrorism' and the 'Comprehensive Convention on International Terrorism' in the UN. The underpinning of both these conventions is that it 'urges all nations to pass law domestically that 'makes all acts of terrorism for political purposes' unjustifiable 'irrespective of political, philosophical, ideological and racial considerations.' Hence, while both countries have refused to negotiate their respective disputes of Chechnya and Kashmir with the peoples' representatives, both countries want to associate the resistance movements raging in the two regions with terrorism.[12]

During the Russian President, Vladimir Putin's visit to India in December 2002, the two countries signed a 'Memorandum of Understanding on Cooperation in Combating Terrorism'. As a result, a Joint Working Group on 'Combating International Terrorism' was also established which held its first meeting in Moscow on September 29-30, 2003. Both sides also 'agreed to set up a panel of experts to fight terror' and to 'share information between their security agencies, exchange equipment and help each other with training.' This is helping both countries to share each others' experiences in quelling the uprisings in their respective restless regions. Russia's acquiescence could not be ruled out in the handing over of a few Taliban elements to India, who were captured by the Northern Alliance after the fall of the Taliban regime in Afghanistan in November 2001.[13]

Joint stand on Kashmir and Chechnya

The Joint Statement issued at the end of their Summit-level talks in New Delhi in October 2000, also expressed the position of the two countries on the restive situation in Kashmir and Chechnya. The Statement appreciated the 'measures taken by India in combating terrorism and ushering in normalcy in the State of Jammu and Kashmir'. It explicitly demanded an end to 'cross-border terrorism' for the resumption of bilateral talks between India and Pakistan. On the Chechen and Kashmir issue, both countries hold similar views: that the violent movements of self-determination being waged in both the regions are acts of terrorism. Furthermore, both countries link these self-determination movements with outside support which target their sovereignty and territorial integrity. President Putin's address to Indian Parliament in which he said that "the same people are organising terrorist attacks from the Philippines to Kosovo, including Kashmir, Afghanistan and Russia's Northern Caucasus"[14] are an ample proof of their unanimity of views on Kashmir and Chechnya.

During the Indian Prime Minister Vajpayee's visit to Russia in November 2001, President Putin stated that, he would urge the US President George Bush, to include 'Pakistan-backed insurgents in Kashmir' and Chechen 'rebels' in Russia on the list of terrorists to be targeted by the US-led coalition.[15]

On the eve of the Russian President's visit to India in December 2002, the Russian Foreign Minister, Igor Ivanov, wrote in an article published in a Russian newspaper Roosiiskaya Gazeta reiterating this connection between insurgency in Kashmir and Chechnya. He stated: "today ties between the terrorists operating in Chechnya, Afghanistan, Kashmir, the Philippines and other parts of the world have become a generally accepted fact. It is a well-known fact that they have undergone training in the camps and are using similar crime tactics and methods.' Further that "for the same reasons, Russia treats with understanding the concern of India over the penetration of groups of militants through the Line of Control into the state of Jammu and Kashmir. It shares the opinion about the need for the fulfillment by Pakistan of the obligations assumed to liquidate the terrorist infrastructure on the territory under its control."[16]

The Russian Ambassador to India, Alexander Kadakin, also wrote in an article published in Nezavisimaya Gazeta in its issue of December 3, 2002, and addressed the pertinent aspect of the Kashmiri peoples' struggle for self-determination in terms of dismissal by equating 'liberation struggle' with 'international banditry'. He advised that 'foreign policy should not succumb to the temptation of ignoring this, and that Pakistan, by completely and unconditionally fulfilling its obligations to end 'cross-border terrorism' and destroy the terrorist infrastructure within its territory, would open up possibilities for the resumption of a long overdue peaceful dialogue between India and Pakistan'.[17]

The present position of Russia on Kashmir is very favourable to India in the sense that Russia, as a major power and permanent member of UNSC, is bending over backwards to consolidate past friendship, and make strategic partnership a reality. While Pakistan officially recognises the Chechen dispute as an internal matter of the Russian Federation, and avoids giving harsh statements on this account, Russia's unflinching support to India on Kashmir will undoubtly harm Pakistan's principled stand on the Kashmir dispute.

Coordination on Afghanistan

Both countries regard Afghanistan as the hub of instability in the South and Central Asian region. Russia is apprehensive of an instable Afghanistan, since it may destabilise the Central Asian region as a whole, thereby impacting on Russia itself. India believes that the Kashmiri 'insurgents' have a strong nexus with Afghanistan, and in the past received their training in camps in Afghanistan.

Apart from the so-called terrorist threats facing Russia and India from Afghanistan, the war-ravaged country holds political and economic importance for both Russia and India. According to the former Foreign Secretary of India, the late J.N. Dixit, ideal relations with Afghanistan "are of utmost important to India not only in terms of bilateral equations, but also as an area through which India's economic relations and cooperation in other fields with the Central Asian republics will be facilitated."[18] On its part, Russia would like to maintain its cold war era influence on Afghanistan to strengthen its political and economic grip on its southern belly – the Central Asian states. Russia is apprehensive that after attaining independence from it in 1991, these Central Asian States are drifting apart.

The decision to set up a 'Joint Working Group (JWG) on Afghanistan' showed the extent of seriousness of the two countries on collaborating on that front. The fact that both countries have held six sessions of JWG on Afghanistan during the year 2000-2003, speaks of their close collaboration and joint stand on developments taking place *vis-à-vis* Afghanistan. In the post-Taliban Afghanistan, both countries are cooperating to gain maximum advantage from the evolving situation in the war-torn country, and aimed at excluding Pakistan from any future say in the Afghan affairs. During Vajpayee's visit to Russia in November 2001, the Russian President, Vladimir Putin, said in a press conference that India would be more actively involved in the 6+2 mechanism earlier evolved in the mid-1990s to bring peace to Afghanistan – that comprises Pakistan, Iran, China, Tajikistan, Turkmenistan, Uzbekistan, Russia and the US. Both countries also ruled out any future role for the remnants of Taliban in any future Afghanistan government. The Moscow Declaration on International Terrorism' signed by the two countries in November 2002 emphasised "the necessity to avert the spilling of the conflict beyond the boundaries of one region, to prevent further extension of terrorism." Both countries emphasised on maintaining effective interaction in the framework of JWG on Afghanistan. According to the Russian Foreign Minister, Igor Ivanov, "a continual confidential dialogue on Afghan problem is being conducted between us."

During Vajpayee's visit to Russia in November 2003, both countries agreed to increase the frequency of air connections between the two. Also, India agreed to give Russia "fifth freedom rights to Kabul from India subject to the agreement of the Afghan government." The present arrangement is to facilitate Indian movement between New-Delhi and Kabul, since at present, India has no air links or flight rights over Pakistani territory,

Convergence of interests in central Asia

In the Joint Statement issued at the end of summit-level talks between the two leaders in Moscow in November 2001, both sides expressed a deep concern "over the threat to the security and stability in Central Asia posed by international terrorism and religious extremism." Both sides agreed that "regional cooperation can play an important role in the stabilisation of the situation in the Central Asian region."[19] Hence, with the tacit approval of Russia, India has expanded its presence in the region in the shape of providing military assistance and training to the armed forces of Central Asian States (CAS). India has opened a military base in Farkhor, Tajikistan. India realises the importance of Central Asia's market, and is endeavouring to capture its share. The North-South Corridor agreed upon by India, Iran and Russia will go a long way in integrating Indian economy with that of the CAS. Iran's land links to CAS are to be expanded and utilised to carry Indian goods to CAS.

A Drive for multi-polarity and strategic stability

The Declaration of Strategic Partnership issued during the October 2000 visit of Russian President Putin to India and the Joint Statement released thereafter supported the establishment of "a multi-polar world based on sovereign equality of all states." The Joint Statement, while emphasising the recognition of 'legitimate security interest of all states,' expressed its "determined opposition to the unilateral use or threat of use of force in violation of the UN Charter, and to intervention in the internal affairs of other states, including under the guise of humanitarian intervention." The recently established India-Russia Joint Working Group on Global Challenges also held its first meeting in New Delhi in October 2003, to exchange views on global challenges, and to address these challenges in a concerted and comprehensive manner.[20] While identifying transnational terrorism as the main challenge which requires collective action, both countries discussed the prevailing situation in US-occupied Iraq, Afghanistan, Central and South Asia. Also, both countries went a step further by issuing a Political Declaration on Global Challenges and Threats to World Security and Stability, whereby both countries agreed to coordinate their positions on various regional and international issues.

Inter-institutional sooperation between state institutions

Both countries established the 'Eminent Persons Group' during President Putin's visit to India in October 2000, with the objective of 'rendering assistance' and 'preparing recommendations' to strengthen bilateral relations, and cooperate on regional and international issues'.[21] Also, both sides have institutionalised interaction between the National Security Council of India (NSCI) and Security Council of the Russian Federation (SCRF) on a regular basis through a protocol signed in April 2000. Two Working Groups have been established under the aegis of the NSCI and SCRF: one on Regional Security; and, the other on International Terrorism. The working groups conducted regularly have been successful in yielding the expected results between the two countries.

Parliamentary cooperation also constitutes an important facet of Indo-Russian ties, aimed at forging contacts across the political spectrum of both the countries. A Charter of the India-Russia Inter-Parliamentary Commission was signed in Moscow in November 1998. The first session of the Inter-Parliamentary Commission was held in India in February 2000, when Russia's State Duma Speaker, Gennady Selezynev, visited India. There is also active cooperation between the Election Commissions of the two countries, the Comptroller and Auditor Generals of India and Russia, and the Judicial Authorities of the two countries.[22] The visit of former Prime Minister Vajpayee to Russia in November 2003, has also witnessed the signing of a protocol between their respective foreign ministries on joint publication of bilateral archive documents as well.

Collaboration on multilateral forums

Russia, along with China and Central Asian States, is a member of the Shanghai Cooperation Organisation (SCO), established to fight the menace of the militancy and separatism in the CIS and China. India and Pakistan, though not members of the SCO, are striving for the same. Russia is also lending full support to India's membership of the SCO.[23] While Pakistan is anxious to join the SCO, and its application has been backed by China, Russia wants priority to be given to India to avoid it being equated with Pakistan. Russia and India are also collaborating in the UN within the framework of the Comprehensive Convention on International Terrorism, and the Convention for the Suppression of Acts of Nuclear Terrorism. In the Joint Statement signed in December 2002, during President Putin's visit to India, Russia expressed its strong support 'to India as a deserving and strong candidate for the permanent membership in an expanded UNSC. (United Nations Security Council).[24]

Scientific and Technological Cooperation

At present, Russia and India have a scientific and technological cooperation arrangement under the Integrated Long Term Programme of Cooperation in Science and Technology (till 2010), which is a continuation of the earlier Integrated Long Term Programme of Cooperation in Science and Technology (ILTP) signed between India and the FSU in July 1987. The Declaration on Strategic Partnership signed in October 2000 laid clear emphasis on strengthening close cooperation within the framework of the India-Russian Inter-Governmental Commission (IRIGC) for Trade, Economic, Scientific, Technological and Cultural Cooperation. Twelve Working Groups were established under the IRIGC, covering different spheres. These are as follows: (i) Trade and Economic Cooperation; (ii) Power and Non-conventional Sources of Energy; (iii) Petroleum (Oil Industry); (iv) Ferrous and Non-Ferrous Metallurgy; (v) Science and Technology; (vi) Culture; (vii) Coal; (viii) Information Technology; (ix) Environment and Natural Resources; (x) Pharmaceuticals; (xi) Cooperation between Regions; (xii) and Cooperation in Civil Aviation.[25]

During President, Putin's visit to India in December 2002, both countries signed a Joint Declaration on Strengthening and Enhancing Economic, Scientific, and Technological Cooperation. The cooperation is meant to impart a new dynamism to this aspect by getting the two sides together at the highest level to agree to certain principles, or a framework, and the contents of the framework and the principles that should govern the efforts of both sides to enhance economic trade.

The scientific and technological cooperation between the two countries is deepening with the course of time. Both countries have earmarked areas where fruitful collaboration is possible, and is aimed at the betterment of their masses. Russia has also expressed its desire to modernise and upgrade several sectors, like thermal power projects, steel mills, and the construction of new power grids. In coal mining, Russia is effectively assisting India in its modernisation of coal mining enterprises by using modern technology. The two countries are also working on joint ventures in the oil and gas industry – which will be implemented in India, Russia and other countries, like Indian investment in Russia's East Siberian oil fields in Sakhalin. Electronics, information technology, pharmaceuticals, biotechnology and civil aviation are some of the areas where Russia wants to be very active and seeks joint ventures with India. Russia has also expressed its desire to provide India with silicon and semi-conductors. In biotechnology,

Russia has expressed its readiness to cooperate in the production of pharmaceuticals, and the supply of poly-vaccines and immuno-biological substances.[26]

Both countries also signed a 'Memorandum of Understanding on Cooperation in the Field of Telecommunication'. They are already collaborating on a joint venture project in providing telecom and internet services for sending large volumes of information using satellites. Both countries also signed a Protocol on Intellectual Property Rights during President Putin's visit to India in December 2002. Apart from this, both countries have also worked out mutually beneficial projects in the field of civil aviation, such as designing light passenger and cargo aircraft.

The Inter-Session Review Meeting of the Indo-Russian Inter-Governmental Cooperation that took place on November 22, 2002, reported that 156 joint research projects in different areas of science and technology have been completed, and 2,500 exchanges have taken place. In the month of November 2003, 87 new projects were identified for cooperation between the two countries. An Indo-Russian Science Centre has been set up in order to enter into joint ventures of Russian scientific institutions for commercialisation of high technology.[27]

There is an Indo-Russian Centre for Advanced Computing Research at the Institute for Computer-Aided Design (ICAD) of the Russian Academy of Sciences in Moscow. The Centre has acquired C-DAC's latest PARAM 10000 supercomputer, which will be used for the development of various software applications of mutual interests by India and Russia.[28] It would engage in academic research, and solicit commercial projects for Third World countries in weather forecasting and computer modeling in various areas. Also, both countries have set up an Indo-Russian Centre for Oceanography, as well as an Indo-Russian Centre for Biotechnology. Also, an International Advanced Research Centre for powder metallurgy and new materials in Hyderabad, and the Bharat Immunological and Biological Corporation Ltd., in Bulandshar has also been established.

Moreover, Russian students are also availing the Indian Technical and Economic Cooperation (ITEC) courses in various faculties in India, since Russia is a partner country of ITEC.[29]

Also, during the state visit of Prime Minister Vajpayee to Russia in November 2003, both countries inked an MOU between the Indian Space Research Organisation (ISRO) and the Russian Aviation and Space Agency Cooperation (Rosaviakosmos) in the Exploration and Use of Outer Space for Peaceful Purposes, that includes Russian assistance in an Indian lunar mission as well. India is also keen to be involved in the development of a new Russian satellite navigation system that also involves the launch and fabrication of satellites. The visit also witnessed the signing of an 'Agreement on Scientific Cooperation and Scientific Exchange' between the Indian Department of Science and Technology and the Russian Academy of Sciences. It calls for bilateral exchange of 200 scientists on annual basis for project-based work, technology transfer, and exploring new avenues of scientific cooperation. During the same visit, two MoUs were signed between the two governments: one related to the establishment of an Indo-Russian Science and Technology Centre for Gas Hydrates Studies at Chennai, India; and the other related to the establishment of the Indo-Russian Centre for Earthquake Research to be set up at the Indian Meteorological Department in New Delhi.

Some of the important Scientific and Technological collaborations and interactions that are in progress and implementation are listed below.

a) The Russian- Indian Centre for Advanced Computing Research (RICCR) was founded in 2000, where from India the International Institute of Information Technology is the major partner. In January 2004 the President of RICCR set up an Institute in Moscow promoted by Institute of Computer Aided Design (ICAD) of Russian Academy of Science and Indian Pune-based Centre for Development of Advanced Computing (CDAC). The institution has the largest installation outside India of PARAM super computer developed by CDAC. Every year ten Russian students will get scholarship in India and 40 students from India will obtain doctorates in Moscow.

b) An agreement was concluded recently during Science and Technology Minister Kapil Sibil's visit to Moscow to set up an Indian Technology Centre in Moscow under the

Technological Partnership Accord signed during President Vladimir Putin's visit to Delhi in 2002. India has the largest Integrated Long Term Programmes (ILTP). Scientific and technological corporation involves thousands of scientists of the best labs and research institutes from both countries. These initiatives survived the collapse of USSR. Several world class cutting-edge technology in India through ILTP including opening the Power Metallurgy Centre in Hyderabad are in operation.

c) The importance of Joint efforts in space exploration was reiterated at the last summit. Two central agreements on space cooperation namely in the field of exploration and use of Outer Space for Peaceful Purposes and on Long Term Cooperation in the Field of Joint Development Operation and Utilisation of Russian Global Navigation Satellite System (GLONASS) were signed, which gives support to mutually beneficial bilateral relations.

d) The Indian industry has already identified areas of mutual interest such as information technology, pharmaceuticals, telecommunications, hydro carbons, energy and power and production of a medium size passenger-cum-cargo aircraft.

e) An MOU on Intellectual Propriety Rights signed between India and Russia has removed a major stumbling block in Scientific and Technological collaboration.

f) Former President Abdul Kalam's visit to Russia in the year 2005 marked a high point in Indo-Russian high-tech collaboration. President Kalam has very old ties with Researchers and technical staff of Russian Academies. He was paid glowing tributes by Rector of Moscow University Academician Sadovnitchy.[30]

Trade and Economic Cooperation

At present, non-military trade between Russia and India stands at roughly US$1.7 billion annually. Major Indian exports to Russia are drugs and pharmaceuticals, tea, coffee, rice, leather products, food products, processed minerals, cotton yarn fabric, etc. Indian imports from Russia comprises fertilisers, newsprint and paper products, iron and steel, non-ferrous metals, organic chemicals, etc. While international investment is needed to boost the economies of both countries, Russia and India are encouraging their private entrepreneurs to invest in sectors that are mutually beneficial. An Indian firm, ONGC Videsh Limited, has recently concluded an agreement to invest US$ 1.7 billion in the Sakhalin-1 oil and gas proje.t. The signing of the Intergovernmental Agreement on Civil Aviation has also opened up broad prospects for the development of bilateral ties in civil aviation.[31]

The Confederation of Indian Industries signed an agreement with the Russian Union of Industrialists and Entrepreneurs on setting up of representative offices in Moscow and New Delhi respectively. The EXIM (Export-Import) Bank of India signed an agreement to extend a credit line of US$ 10 million with the Vnesheconombank of the Russian Federation. The State Bank of India and the Central Bank of Russia also reached agreement with the Central Bank of Russia for setting up a branch in Moscow.[32]

According to government officials, Russian firms have expressed interest in participating in the upgradation of Indian steel plants. Russian companies have recently shown interest in investing in the Indian power sector, metallurgy industry and railways. During the visit of a delegation to India in the year 2002, some Russian companies have initiated talks with their Indian counterparts in the field of telecommunications, information technology and electronics.[33]

Also, both countries along with Iran have signed an agreement on opening a North-South Corridor, which connects Mumbai with Russia's St. Petersburg via Bandar Abbass. The corridor is expected to handle 15-20 million tons of freight annually, with the trade turnover pegged at US$10 billion. It will cut the mileage from 16,129 km to just 6,245 km. It will also cut transport time by at least 10-12 days, and transport costs by about 15-20 per cent.[34]

While both countries are striving to boost their economic relations further, there are several factors that will impact upon their economic relations. At present, India is paying the Russian Federation Rs. 3,000 crores as external debt it owed to the FSU. Russia is not a member of the WTO. Hence, India may not be able to give it the same trading status as it is bound to give to WTO member countries. Also, Russia's banking and financial system is not in compliance with India or other developed countries. Moreover, its investment laws are not based on equity basis that may discourage future Indian investments in Russia economic sectors.

Cultural Cooperation

The October 2000 Declaration on Strategic Partnership laid great emphasis on promoting cultural cooperation, and people-to-people contact. India's most extensive cultural, academic, scientific, educational, sports and other exchanges are carried under the Cultural Exchange Programmes (CEP). Under this arrangement, both countries organised the 'Days of Russian Culture'; the 'Days of Indian Culture'; 'Days of Moscow'; and the 'Days of New Delhi' in their respective countries on alternate basis in the years 1995, 1996, 1998, and 1999 respectively.[35]

Exchanges have also been taking place on a regular basis between academics and scholars of the two countries in the shape of seminars, round-tables, conferences etc. A Mahatma Gandhi Chair of Indian Philosophy was formally inaugurated in February 1999, at the Institute of Philosophy, Russian Academy of Sciences. The visit of Indian Prime Minister Vajpayee, to Russia in November 2001, also witnessed the signing of four agreements on promoting education and research at four leading Russian institutes: Jawaharlal Nehru Cultural Centre and the Institute of Oriental Studies at the Russian Academy of Science; the St. Petersburg State University; the Kazan State University; and the Far Eastern National University in Vladivostok.[36]

Regional Cooperation

Both sides attach great importance to the development of ties between the regions of their respective countries. In this connection, a Working Group for Regional Cooperation under the India-Russia Inter-Governmental Agreement on the 'Principles of Cooperation between the Government of the States and Union Territories of the Republic of India and the bodies of Executive Authority of the Constituent Entities of the Russian Federation' was signed during the visit of President Putin to India in October 2000. Under these agreements, partner-relations and cooperation between the Astrakhan region in the Russian Federation and the

Gujarat State in India were established When Prime Minister Vajpayee visited Russia in November 2001.[37] Also, a Protocol on behalf of the State of Karnataka and Russia's Samara region to enhance trade, economic, technological and cultural cooperation was signed during President Putin's visit to India in December 2002.

Military Technical Cooperation

The military ties between India and Russia have a very long history which is full of mutual understanding and based on the concept of strategic partnership. Of course market situation forces these to change from time to time taking into consideration the most perspective trends in the development of Indo-Russian military and technology cooperation. There is increasing awareness on both sides on willingness to incorporate latest achievements of other countries such as France and Israel, etc. Su-30MK1 is an example of such cooperation, wherein Sukhoy Designing office worked closely with France's SNECMA and Russia's NPO Saturn over working or Sa M 146 engines. Integration of our armament industries in the military technical cooperation and bringing diverse international skills together to enhance capabilities of the product will reduce the costs by way of sharing the investments in R&D.[38]

Both countries are actively engaged in enhancing and developing inherent capabilities and potential of Su 30 MK1, Multirole Combat Aircraft (MRCA). Indian research and development agencies like Electronic R & D Establishment (LRDE) and Defence Avionics Research Establishment (DARE) have joined hands with Rosoboron Export and V.V. Tikhomirov Scientific Research Institute of Instrument Building (Tikhomirov NIIP) along with India-Russia Venture BrahMos Aerospace. It is expected that by 2010 the first totally-built Su30 Mk1 will roll out from India's Hindustan Aeronautics Ltd. (HAL) production facility at NASHIK. It will be equipped with new active phased-array airborne radar called the IRBIS, being jointly produced at a cost of US Dollars 160 million. The Su30 MK1 is capable to carry 2.5 tonnes BraMos missile along with other deadly ordnance.[39] With further strengthening of aircraft wings the MRCA it should be able to carry up to three BrahMos missiles.

BrahMos is a shining example of a joint venture in defence Technology. The agreement to design, develop, produce and market a multi-role supersonic cruise missile was signed in 1998 between Russian Federal State unitary Enterprise (NPCM) and India's state owned "Defence Research and Development Organisation (DRDO). The system has been accepted by Indian and Russian armed Forces Ramjet technology from Yakhont and improved onboard guidance and navigation from Indian missile programmed, basically sees the synergy from the two sides. The production of the cruise missile does not violate obligations under MTCR. The display of this missile in numerous DEFEXPO's (Defence Exposures) around the world has evinced keen interest. It is expected that Chile may be its first customer. India's Defence Minister Mr. Pranab Mukherjee recently visited Chile (November2005) and had this item on his agenda.[40]

The modernisation of Admiral Gorshkov renamed the Vikramaditya is another example of successful international collaboration. Of interest could be development of T-72 M1M main battle tank, the revamped version of T-72 with the MSTA[40] 5 self-propelled gun and enhancement of range and better accuracy of smirch multiple-launch rocket systems are the features of this up gradation. This project has competition from Ukraine where similar up gradation is also possible.[41]

The current Indo-Russian dialogue on Defence Technical collaborations / purchase of equipment include co-production of weapon systems and platforms on investment-sharing basis like fifth generation fighter aircraft and advanced Amur Class submarine as discussed between visiting Russian Defence Minister Sergei Ivanov and the Indian counterpart Mr. Pranab Mukharjee during their meeting at Delhi on 16 October 2005. Earlier the Russian Navy Commander Vladimir Kuriyedov in July 2005 at St. Petersburg had indicated the advantages of this fourth stealth type AMUR with most modern weaponry. Admiral Verfi shipyard at St.Petersburg is spearheading this project.[42]

The problems that the Indian Armed Forces face vis-à-vis speedy supply of spare parts and maintenance and repair support from Russia are being progressively addressed. Suitable clauses are being built into the new contracts. These envisage creation of Military technical maintenance centers in India. Contracts for

GORSHKOV, SU 30 MK1, BrahMos and T-90 s tanks have these provisions incorporated. These facilities may also be extended to other foreign countries holding comparable Russian equipment.

The creation of Rosoboron Service (India) Ltd. is a first ever unique joint venture consequent to a decree by the Russian President. It involves eight Russian defence manufacturers/ vendors who have joined hands with an Indian company in private sector. This company will operate a bonded warehouse to stock Russian defence equipment. This venture is manned by skilled ex-servicemen of Indian Armed Forces. The mandated activities of the company, registered in India, range from repairs and maintenance of systems to spare parts supply and training of personnel. Initially to meet needs of the Indian Navy this company will later on take on the service/maintenance of Russian–supplied assets of the Indian Air Force.[43]

This arrangement was insisted upon by Indian Navy during negotiations for Gorshkov deal. This is a step in the right direction but more needs to be done in this direction both in letter and spirit. There are estimates that hundred Russian defence production facilities are kept in operation by Indian defence contracts . In the next five years India is likely to purchase arms worth US$ 14 billion. A major portion of this may come from Russia. The Indo-Russian military exercises in October 2005 have been a step in consolidation of relationship. The naval exercises in the Eastern sea off Vishakahptnam had the front line ships of both countries take part in manoeuvres and synchronised missile and antisubmarine weapon's firing. The Russian ships were under the command of Rear Admiral Sergey Viktrovich of the Pacific Fleet. Similarly para-drop exercises of men and armaments in Pokharan by Indian Air Force and Indian Army were witnessed closely by the Russian Defence Minister. It is a known fact that India which went ahead with the deal for procurement of aircraft carrier *Admiral Gorshkov* from Russia in 2004 and which was to be inducted in the armada of Indian Navy by August 2008 shall now be delivered only in 2012. over and above quite contrary to international norms the Russian side has asked India to pay up additional US$ 1.2 Billion from the value contracted initially which leaves India with no option but to buckle under such pressure and accept these terms.[44]

Nuclear Cooperation

An Inter-Governmental Agreement (IGA) on the construction of a 2000 MW Koodankulam Nuclear Power Station worth US$ 2.6 billion in India was signed between then Prime Minister, Rajiv Gandhi, and then Soviet President, Mikhail Gorbachev, in November 1988. The supplement to the 1988 IGA was signed in New Delhi in June 1998, and was further augmented by an MOU for the construction of the plant, signed during Prime Minister Vajpayee's visit to Russia in November 2001. However, details of the MOU have not been made public. Another significant aspect of this cooperation is that Russia will finance half the cost of the project, whose total cost is estimated at Rs. 131.7 billion.[45] A Memorandum of Understanding in the Peaceful Uses of Nuclear Energy was also signed during President Putin's visit to India in October 2000.

However, Russia's military and nuclear cooperation with India is a cause of concern for the South Asian states. Russia is providing nuclear technology to India in sheer disregard of Nuclear Suppliers Group (NSG) regulations, knowing well that Indian nuclear installations are not covered under the IAEA safeguards. Also, Russia is selling military hardware to India to the tune of US$ 2 billion annually, which is creating an imbalance in conventional armament in the South Asian region, and could result in an arms race in the region. The statement of Russian Atomic Energy Ministry during the visit of Indian then Prime Minister Vajpayee to Russia that "It is high time to review bans on nuclear cooperation with India imposed in 1992 by the Nuclear Suppliers Group," is highly alarming. The fact that Indian nuclear installations are outside the nuclear safeguards of IAEA is a serious cause of concern for the international community, because of Indian hegemonistic ambitions in the region based on military conventional, as well as nuclear and missile strengths. Also, Russia has proved to be the most imprudent nuclear proliferator in the world through its ambiguous nuclear cooperation with India as well as other countries.[46]

Likewise, since Putin's visit in 2000, Moscow renewed its interest in helping New Delhi boost its civilian atomic energy programme. Now India doesn't have much choice as negotiations with France (a quite desirable partner) didn't bring immediate results. Russia is still not very predictable due to international, mainly, US pressure. In 2000 there were two memorandums signed: the Memorandum of Understanding on Peaceful Nuclear Energy and Declaration on Strategic Partnership but only latter was made public. Russia is concerned to act in the framework of nuclear export mechanism - the Nuclear Suppliers Group (NSG). It restrained itself by the Federal Law "On export Control" adopted in 1999 and also by organising the Export Control Commission which was supposed to check compatibility of Russian bilateral and multilateral contracts with country's international commitments. Putin made a serious step to facilitate the situation by amending Russian export control legislation. But even with support of France on the question of legitimate transfer of nuclear supplies to India as a subject of possibly relaxed restrictions, Russia had to inform New Delhi "to find a way of getting the Americans on board".[47]

At the same time even being criticised by the West, Russia came to rescue India when China cut supplies of enriched uranium fuel to Tarapur. Moreover, Putin was the first leader to visit Bhabha Atomic Research Center (BARC) after nuclear tests.

The latest Head of Russian MinAtom, A.Rumyantsev, has been very clear in his wish to cooperate with India on nuclear issues. "India is our strategic partner. We want to ensure that there are no reproaches (from the international community) in this regard."[48] He confirmed that Russia was still intending to continue assisting in building nuclear power station despite international concern saying that "We will do our best to participate in India's ambitious programme to generate 20,000 MW of nuclear power by 2020." There are also speculations about Russia helping India in constructing a nuclear reactor for its nuclear submarine and "supplying India with 300-kilometre range Klub class cruise missiles that can be launched under water."[49]

An Overview of Exchange of Visits Till 2007

There have been a large number of important visits/bilateral contacts between India and the Russian Federation. At the level of President/Prime Minister /EAM(External Affairs Minister), these include: EAM's (External Affairs Minister), visit to Moscow in November 1991; Russian President Yeltsin's State visit to India in January 1993; PM's visit to Russia in June-July 1994; Russian PM Chernomyrdin's visit to India in December 1994; EAM's visit to Moscow from May 8-10, 1995 to participate in the Victory-Europe Day celebrations; EAM's (External Affairs Minister), visit to Russia from August 3-6, 1995; Russian FM Primakov's visit to India on March 29-30, 1996; EAM's (External Affairs Minister), visit to Russia from February 9-13, 1997; PM's visit to Russia in March 1997; Russian PM Primakov's visit to India in December 1998, EAM's (External Affairs Minister) visit to Moscow in May 1999 as well as in June 2000; President Putin's State Visit to India in October 2000; Foreign Minister Igor Ivanov's visit to India in May 2001; Raksha Mantri/EAM's visit in June 2001; PM was on a State Visit to Russia from November 4-7, 2001; and Foreign Minister Mr. Igor Ivanov visited India from February 3-4, 2002. Russian Minister of Industry and Science & Technology Mr. Ilya Klebanov visited India on 21-22 November 2002 to hold the Inter-Session Review Meeting of the Indo-Russian Inter-Governmental Commission, which is Co-Chaired from the Indian side by EAM. (External Affairs Minister), President Putin visited India in December 2002.[50]

Some of the important exchange of visits by the dignatories between the two countries are explained as under.

President Putin's Visit to India: December 2004[51]

President Putin's visit to India in December 2004 has taken place at an opportune time when there seems to be an underlying process of re-assessment of options, both in Russia and India. President Putin can be said to be seriously attempting to re-build the strategic partnership that existed between former Soviet Union and India during the cold war period. Russia had let this partnership glow in the post-cold war period of the 1990's. The above is evidenced by the composition of the Russian President's high-powered delegation. Besides President Putin, it included:

1. Deputy Prime Minister, Alexander Zhukov.
2. Foreign Minister, Sergei Lavrov.
3. Defence Minister Sergei Ivanov.
4. Minister for Information Technology and Communications.

5. Director General of Russian Atomic Agency,
6. Russian Industry Heads.

The Russian Defence Minister had arrived earlier than the President for detailed two-day discussions with the Indian Defence Minister. The summit meeting between President Putin and Indian Prime Minister Dr. Manmohan Singh produced:

- Joint declaration emphasizing the strategic partnership between India and Russia.
- Ten MOUs and agreements covering bilateral cooperation in the fields of outer space exploration, energy, navigation, visa services and banking.

Major points that have emerged on this count during the Russian President's visits are: [52]

- Russia and India will move from a 'buyer-seller' relationship to an expanded joint research and development and joint production of weapon systems'.
- Joint investment in the Brahmos cruise missile will be enhanced for grater production.
- Both countries will explore joint production of fifth generation strike combat aircraft.
- Joint air-borne troops' exercise will be held.
- Intellectual property rights agreement in relation to defence production would be finalised within five months.
- Agreements on upgradation of existing Russian weapon systems in India were signed.
- Supply of Russians spares for India's future requirements were discussed and procedures streamlined.
- The emphasis on joint research development and production of weapon systems is notable in many ways.

Visit of Indian Prime Minister in December 2005

India's Prime Minister, Dr Manmohan Singh visited Russia in the first week of December 2005 for the annual summit meeting with the Russian President. Besides a long meeting with President Putin, the Indian Prime Minister in the course of his three day visit, also had discussions with other Russian officials. The Indian

Prime Minister's visit to Russia took place after four months of his historic summit meeting with President Bush of the United States in mid-July 2005. The July 18, 2005 Indo-US Summit meeting becomes, therefore, a contextual frame against the backdrop of which the Russian visit of the Indian Prime Minister can be comparatively reviewed.

Indo-Russian Agreements Signed during Indian Prime Minister's Visit:

- India and Russia signed the following agreements during the December 2005 visit to Moscow:[53]
- Reciprocal Protection of Intellectual Property Rights in Military Technical Cooperation.
- Space Exploration Cooperation Agreement.
- Agreement on Cooperation in the Field of Solar Physics and Solar Terrestrial Relationships.
- Agreement on Implementation of Programme for Military and Technical Cooperation up to 2010.
- No agreements seem to have been signed in the field of trade and economic cooperation. The India request for easy visa issuance to Indian business leaders was not addressed.

Indian Prime Minister's Visit to Russia Reviewed: Major Observations:

A review of the visit leads to the following major observations:[54]

- No official or media hype attended the visit of the Indian Prime Minister. It went through as a routine annual summit meeting.
- Indian expectations that Russia may be more forthcoming on Indian's civil nuclear energy programme requirements did not materialise.
- The Russian President toed the American line that any progress in this sphere would depend on India's agreement to adhere to conditions stipulated by USA and the Nuclear Suppliers Group.

- There was a total absence of geo-political or economic content in the two leaders' discussions, going by media reports.
- The agreements signed during the visit were confined to defence and scientific cooperation.

President Putin's Visit to India (January 2007)

It would be fair to point out that in the run-up to President Putin's visit to India, there was a noticeable lack of hype in the Indian media and analytical coverage by the strategic community. It was only on the eve of President Putin's visit that media and analysts attention turned towards this significant event. It was as if this visit was going to be devoid of any significant gains for India. As it turned out, the Russian President's visit to India turned out to be strategically significant for India and Russia too, in more ways than one. The January 2007 visit to India by President Putin has helped Russia to reclaim a significant focus in India's public strategic consciousness in multiple ways as follows:[55]

- President Putin's visit in January 2007 was his first visit to India after the Indo-US Nuclear deal was signed.
- Russia's strategic partnership with India became more visible in its broadest spectrum.
- India's political leaders constant emphasis during this visit of the Russia-India Strategic Partnership as time-tested, reliable and marked by continuity would invariably throw up comparisons with the evolving strategic partnership with the United States.
- Comparisons would also be inevitable of the Indo-US Nuclear Deal with Russia-India Nuclear Cooperation both existing now and in future.
- The very selection of President Putin to be honored as Chief Guest at Indian Republic Day celebrations in 2007 was a gesture to symbolise the importance India attaches to the Russia-India Strategic Partnership.

Conclusion

Indo-Russia relations have greatly expanded in scope in the post-cold war era. Although their relations encompass social, economic, political, geostrategic and defence collaboration, However, security cooperation still remains the dominant aspect of their relationship, with non-traditional threats, like terrorism, narco-trafficking etc., are now part of the traditional notions of security dominant during the cold war era. While both countries have failed to suppress the movements for self-determination being waged in Chechnya and Kashmir, they in turn have focused their energies on getting these freedom movements equated with terrorism. Hence, cooperation on the issue of terrorism will intensify with the passage of time. Both countries are also coordinating their policies on regional issues. Russia is concerned about the evolving situation in Afghanistan, and feels nervous regarding the prospects of Afghanistan falling back into a spiral of anarchy and lawlessness. For Russia, a stable Afghanistan is necessary to keep its soft underbelly – the Central Asian Region—in stable conditions.

Taking advantage of the post- September 11 worldwide concern over global terrorism, India has anchored itself firmly in the Central Asian Region. According to an Indian author, "Russia is interested in the development of cooperation between India and Central Asian States, as a means to counterbalance the influence in Central Asia of neighbouring Islamic countries, as well as the US. India, for its part, is concerned to counter the influence of its arch-rival, Pakistan, in Central Asia, believing that Islamabad's close links with Central Asia would enable Pakistan to acquire strategic depth in any future war against India." India has secured a military base in Farkhor, as well as an airbase at Ayni in Tajikistan, by taking advantage of the apprehensions expressed by the Central Asian States regarding Islamic militancy. India is also imparting training to the armed forces of Central Asian States. However, this could not have happened without Russian consent.

Russia's proposal of a 'strategic triangle' between Russia, India and China is meant to create a world order based on multi-polar system. At present, both China and India have strong economic ties with the US, while Russia is also striving to establish strong economic relations with the US, especially its ongoing energy dialogue with the US to become the leading oil exporter to the US. Therefore, neither of the three – China, Russia and

India—are willing to form any such loose alliance based on challenging the US hegemony in world affairs at the expense of deteriorating their bilateral relations with the US. Hence, in terms of strategic payoffs, this partnership based on the thoughts of 'strategic triangle' will yield them enhanced benefits of bilateral cooperation with each other. However, the proposed strategic triangle can act as a bulwark against the threat of Islamic extremism.

Moreover, India in the post-cold war era has a desire to establish strategic relations with the Western countries, especially the US. The address of the then Indian Deputy Prime Minister, L. K. Advani, at the World Affairs Council during his visit to the US in June 2003, is worth mentioning in which he said that both US and India are 'partners in the fight against Jehadi terrorism,' and that "a strategic partnership can become a reality only if the major strands in the relationship – political, economic, and military – are tightly woven together." Also, India is in the process of diversifying its heavy military hardware dependence on Russia aimed at purchasing weapons from the US, Israel, and other Western European countries. There is a strong believe that Israel may surpass Russia as the biggest supplier of military hardware to India in few years.

Also, the establishment of a Joint Defence Policy Group (DPG) between India and the US in November 2001, is testament to the fact that both India and the US want to co-opt each other in the fight against what they perceive as 'Islamic extremism.' The military exercises held between the two sides in the past few years, such as the Malabar naval exercises of 1992, 1995, 1996, 2002, 2003 are an ample proof. Also, Indo-US joint military exercise in Alaska (namely, Geronimo Thrust 02) in October 2002 was a step towards closer military training cooperation.

Against this backdrop of Indo-US burgeoning relationship, Russia and Indian relations have the potential to decline from this present state of a stable relationship. India, while striving to establish strategic relations with the US, is also endeavouring to win Russia and other regional players on its side through the so-called myth of a 'strategic triangle,' with a view to containing Pakistan. Russia is supportive of Indian positions on all outstanding issues between the latter and Pakistan. It is really ironic that while India is fighting its 'War on Kashmir', whose war is Russia fighting in Kashmir? Russia is bending over backwards to please India, and the present partnership seems to be driven more by Russia's political opportunism for economic benefits, and India's economic and military needs.

Furthermore, the assurances extended by the Putin administration during former Prime Minister Vajpayee's visit to Russia from November 11-14, 2003, that third party mediation on Kashmir was not a solution to the problem, and that Russia would not countenance Islamabad's anti-India tirade is a testament to the fact that Russia's policy towards South Asia is heavily tilted in India's favour. Such a policy is tantamount to disturbing the regional peace. Russia should realise that constructive engagement with Pakistan is more fruitful in Afghanistan, than aligning itself with India. In a nutshell, India and Russia are in the process of institutionalising their relations. The formation of various working groups to monitor developments on political, economic, science and technology and cultural fronts will go a long way in strengthening their bilateral relations. Warmth in Indo-Russia relations depends to a greater degree on how India balances itself between its increasing desire to ally with the US, Israel and the West, and maintain traditional relations with the Russian Federation.

References

1. Anita Inder Singh, 'India's Relations with Russia and Central Asia', *International Affairs,* RIIA, Vol. 17, No. 1, 1995, p.87.
2. John Cherian, 'A Strategic Partnership' *Frontline,* Vol. 17, Issue 21, October 14-27, 2000, p.43.
3. Ibid.
4. 'Russia, China, India: A New Strategic Triangle for a Cold War?', *http://carlisle-www.army.mil/usawc/Parameters/01winter/rahm.htm*
5. Ibid.
6. Bunn Nagara, 'Russia-India in New Convergence', *www.southreview.com,* P-11
7. Anuradha M. Chenoy, 'A Defining Moment', *Frontline,* Vol. 17, Issue 21, October 14-27, 2000.
8. 'Moscow Declaration Between India and Russia on International Terrorism', *http://pib.nic.in/archive/irelong/1yr2001.html*

9. 'Putin, India Vow to Fight Terror', *www.in.news.yahoo.com /021204/ 137/1ysp1.html*
10. Muralidhar Reddy, 'The Pakistan Card', *Frontline,* Vol.17, Issue 21, October 14-27, 2000, p. 65.
11. 'Russia for US Ban on J&K, Chechen Terrorists', *www.hindustantimes.com/nonfram/071101/detfro01.asp*
12. Ibid.
13. Igor Ivanov, 'Russia and India: Together in the Struggle Against International Terrorism', *Rossiiskaya Gazeta,* December 2, 2002, p. 11. *www.ln.mid.ru/brp-4.nsf*
14. Ibid. p.13.
15. Ibid., p.14.
16. Alexander Kadakin, 'Moscow Does Not Foist Itself as a Mediator. The Strategic Partner is the Optimal Model of Foreign Policy Cooperation between Russia and India', *Nezavisimaya Gazeta,* December 3, 2002, p. 87. *www.ln.mid.ru. brp_14.nsf*
17. Lt. General Jasbir Singh, *Indian Defence Yearbook 2000,* Nartaj publishers, 17 Rajpur road, Dehra Dun, India, January 2000, p-54.
18. 'India, Russia Agree Over Terror, Afghanistan', *The Times of India,* November 6, 2001.
19. 'Joint Statement', *www.pib.nic.in/archieve/lreleng/lyr2001/rnov 2001.html*
20. 'First Meeting of the India-Russia Joint Working Group on Global Challenges', *www.ln.mid.ru/brp-4.nsf*
21. 'Press Release', November 6, 2002, *www.pibm.nic.in/archieve/ Ireleng.html*
22. Ibid.
23. 'Bilateral Relations between India and the Russian Federation', *www.meadev.nic.in/foreign/newsrussia.htm*
24. Ibid.
25. An Interview given by the Russian President, Vladimir Putin, to an Indian Newspaper *The Hindu* and Television Channel 'Star TV', the Kremlin, Moscow, November 28, 2002, *www.mid.ru/bl.nsf*
26. 'India, Russia 'Rejoice' in Each Other's Strength', *http:// www.thehindu.com/thehindu/2003/ 02/23/stories/20030223033 70900.htm*
27. 'India-Russia Joint Statement', *www.meadev.nic.in/ speeches/ 4decdelhi-jointstmt.htm*

28. 'Bilateral Relations Between India and the Russian Federation', *www.meadev.nic.in/foreign/newsrussia.htm*
29. 'The Russian Roulette Part II', *http://www.indinetwork.com/indinewsport/joymain7.html*
30. 'Special Media Briefing on the Eve of President of the Russian Federation, Vladimir Putin's Visit, held by Shri Kanwal Sibal', *www.meadev.nic.in/news/Special%20Media20%briefing%EvePresident.htm*
31. 'Bilateral Relations Between India and the Russian Federation', *www.meadev.nic.in/foreign/newsrussia.htm*
32. Ibid.
33. 'Press Release', November 6, 2002, *www.pibm.nic.in/archieve/Ireleng.html*
34. Ibid.
35. http://www.pbs.org/wgbh/commandingheights/shared/minitextlo/int_robertrubin.html#6.
36. Ibid.
37. Ibid.
38. 'Prime Minister,Vajpayee's Interview to Special Correspondent, Vladimir Kukikov From Izvestia', December 3, 2003, *www.meadev.nic.in/govt/pm-vladimirkulikov.htm*
39. 'India, Iran, Russia Map Out Trade Route', *www.atimes.com/ind-pak/DF29Df02.html*
40. Bilateral Relations Between India and the Russian Federation, *www.meadev.nic.in/foreign/newsrussia.htm*
41. Ibid.
42. 'India, Russia Ink Pacts on Education, Research', *The Times of India*, November 6, 2001.
43. 'Changing Contours of Indo-Russian Ties', *http://www.rediff.com / news/ 2000/oct/03putin5.htm*
44. 'Russia, China, India: A New Strategic Triangle for a Cold War?', *http://carlisle-www.army.mil/usawc/Parameters/01winter/rahm.htm*
45. 'India to Build Russian-Aided Nuclear Power Plant', *www.hindustantimes.com/nonfram/041101/Dlnat01.asp* Ibid.,
46. Ibid.
47. Ibid.
48. Robert Hewson, "Russia's PGMs Go on Show", *Jane's Defence Weekly*, October 19, 2005.

49. Ibid.
50. http://jamestown.org/publicationsdetails.php?volume_id=2&&issue_id=21.
51. *Deccan Chronicle,* 2004.
52. Ibid.
53. *The Hindu,* September 5, 2005.
54. Ibid.
55. Ibid.

6

Problems and Prospects of Strategic Triangle among India, Russia and China

Introduction

In the first post-cold war decade, the international system has experienced a period of relative peace among the great powers, not seen since the Concert of Europe after the Napoleonic wars nearly two hundred years ago. The United States is enjoying a period of international dominance even greater than that after World War II, and there is no imaginable competitor on the horizon for at least a decade or two. The most economically and technologically advanced countries in Europe and Asia, which aligned with the United States during the cold war, continue to ride the bandwagon of US power. Imminent decisions that the Bush administration will make on key security issues, including nuclear arms reductions national missile defence and further NATO expansion, will have considerable influence in shaping the policies of existing and emerging great powers with ambivalent attitudes towards the United States – notably India, Russia and China. The system may look overwhelmingly unipolar today, but history suggests that such moments are ephemeral, and we should expect and prepare for a more complex and perhaps dangerous multipolarity to emerge in the first quarter of the new century.[1]

India, Russia and China all express support for a multipolar international system not dominated by the United States and rhetoric support for multipolarity has been a staple of joint statements issued in recent years after Russian summits with India and China. So far, the "strategic triangle" concept is yet to be formally coined.[2]

However, India, Russia and China are understood to have a number of converging interests that could add substance to axis talk. All three were disturbed by the Iraq war and protested against what they viewed as a rejection of the rules of the international game. They still back the primacy of the United Nations Security Council in solving crises and support the principle of non-intervention in the internal affairs of other sovereign states. Apart from shared concerns of US dominance, the three have other common interests and mutually reinforcing needs. All three are weary of militant Islamic groups and want stability in Central Eurasia. This shows that the leaders of Russia, India and China sense the need to undertake regular and frequent consultations with each other with a view to fostering a common minimum understanding of global system today as well as the issues on which they can undertake meaningful cooperation. Any serious analysis of international relations today cannot miss out on these new trends which are as yet nascent but can become relevant and noticeable as and when the need arises.[3]

The Background and rationale of "Strategic Triangle" between India, Russia and China

The proposal for a Moscow–Beijing–Delhi 'strategic triangle' originally came from former Russian Prime Minister Yevgeny Primakov during his visit to India in 1998, when he argued that such an arrangement would represent a force for greater regional and international stability. This, however, did not elicit as enthusiastic a response from China and India as Russia had perhaps hoped for. Since then, though the three countries have focused on improving the nature of their bilateral relationships, they have maintained a safe distance from the Primakov proposal.

But, this idea of a 'strategic triangle' took a tangible form when the foreign ministers of Russia, China, and India – Igor Ivanov, Tang Jiaxuan, and Yashwant Sinha – met on the margins of the United Nations General Assembly in New York in September 2002.[4] Despite the fact that nothing concrete emerged out of that meeting, it represented the first major attempt by the three nations to deliberate on world affairs, and has now become a regular feature of interactions among the three states.

Russia has an extremely important role in this process. Russia's loss of power and influence on the world scene has been a major cause of concern for virtually all of Russia's leaders. There has been a growing and pervasive feeling in Russia that it has surrendered its once powerful position on the world stage for a position of little international influence and respect. It is in this respect that Russia has been trying to establish itself as the hub of two bilateral security partnerships that can be used to counteract US power and influence in areas of mutual concern.

While Russia has witnessed a downward slide in its status as a superpower in the last decade, China is a rising power that sees the USA as the greatest obstacle it faces if it is to achieve a pre-eminent position in the global political hierarchy. As a consequence, China recognises the importance of cooperating with Russia to check US expansionism in the world, even if only in the short term. In fact, Kenneth Waltz has gone as far as to argue that 'wrong' US policies towards Russia and China are moving these two states closer to each other and might even lead to the formation of a new balance of power against the USA.[5]

India, on the other hand, has different considerations, as it is still far from becoming a global power of any reckoning. However, India has always tried to voice the concerns of the so-called Third World, strongly arguing for respecting the sovereignty of all countries and opposing the use of force in international politics. Growing concern that the USA is becoming too powerful and unilateral, and that a unipolar US-dominated world is not in the best interests of weaker states like India might make the idea of a 'strategic triangle' attractive for India.[6]

Moreover, all of the three countries also realise that there is enormous potential in the economic, political, military and cultural realms if bilateral relationships among them can be adequately strengthened. And all of then have made some sincere attempts in this regard in the last couple of years. Nevertheless, huge obstacles remain in moving towards a trilateral strategic partnership, making the very idea of a 'strategic triangle' in the context of Russia–China–India interstate relations rather unrealistic.[7]

Russian-China Relations: On a Postive Track

A new era in Sino-Russian relations was ushered in with the breaking up of the Soviet Union and the advent of the post-cold war period. Moreover, as the relations of China and Russia with the USA deteriorated in the late 1990s, the two countries came closer in identifying with each other's foreign policy interests, calling repeatedly for a multipolar and anti-hegemonic world order.[8] Though neither Russia nor China have been ready to openly provoke the USA, it is clear that their target has been its growing power.

China was worried about what it saw as attempts by the USA to interfere in the domestic affairs of other sovereign states. China had to take a strong stand on this issue, as it had grave implications for China's position on Taiwan. Russia, on the other hand, viewed the expansion of NATO right up to its borders with suspicion about the USA's real motives. In a classic diplomatic *quid pro quo,* while China sympathised with earlier Russian objections to NATO's eastward expansion and recognised Chechnya as a domestic issue for Russia, Russia recognised Taiwan and Tibet as integral parts of China.

While there is little doubt that the Sino-Russian rapprochement in the post-cold war period, especially under Boris Yeltsin, has been a result of the changing balance of power in world politics, it is Putin who has tried to diversify the Eurocentric orientation of post-cold war Russian foreign policy. He has focused on establishing and maintaining a web of relations with major Asian powers, thereby trying to temper the assertive dynamic of US dominance, albeit indirectly. However, while Putin has been trying to build a closer relationship with China, he has also been careful enough in crafting the Sino-Russian relationship as a non-alliance, a non-confrontational relationship that targets no third party.

Russian ties with China in the areas of defence and military technology remain central to the overall Sino-Russian relationship. These range from the short-term purchase of Russian weapons by China to long-term cooperation on joint research, development, and production of military equipment, including relatively new technologies for intercontinental ballistic missile and submarine-launched ballistic missile production.[9]

China is the Russian defence industry's largest client, with sales estimated to be between $1 and $2 billion of a total $4 billion of Russian military exports (Kuchins, 2002: 212). Strengthening the bilateral economic relationship has clearly been the focus area for Russia, impressed as it has been during the last couple of years with China's high growth rates. Emphasis, therefore, has been on increasing bilateral trade in goods and services and cooperation in the energy sector. The official trade turnover between the two nations hit $12 billion in 2002, with increasing Chinese demand for Russian industrial and engineering products, civilian nuclear expertise, and oil. China has also supported Russia's attempts at joining the World Trade Organisation, as prioritising trade and economic cooperation remains key for any long-term strategic partnership.

While bilateral concerns remain dominant in Sino-Russian relations, the two countries have also tried to respond to global security concerns by chalking out common strategies. The latest global concerns have been Iraq, Iran, North Korea, and the weakening of the global non-proliferation and arms control regimes. Russia and China are both important players in ensuring the success of any strategies to deal with such concerns. Both have emphasized the centrality of the UN in dealing with these issues, thereby making their displeasure with the USA's unilateral methods explicit (*Putin and Chinese Leaders Pledge Friendship and Caution North Korea on Nuclear Arms*). They have also, time and again, called for building a multipolar, fair and democratic world order based on the universally recognised principles of international law. However, how far they themselves can offer any workable alternative strategies and restrain the USA remains unclear. But, what is undoubtedly clear is that Sino-Russian ties today are more positive and constructive than at any time since the Sino-Soviet alliance of the 1950s.

Indo-Russian Relations: Historically Robust

There are few examples of a relationship between countries that has been as stable as the one between India and Russia. Despite the momentous changes in the international environment following the end of the cold war, there remains a continued convergence of interests that makes it advantageous for both India and Russia to maintain close ties. Barring a fleeting hiccup during Boris Yeltsin's term as Russia's President, New Delhi and Moscow have been extraordinarily successful in nurturing a friction-free relationship that harks back to the Soviet era. Russia's current President, Putin and the Indian Prime Minister had their fifth summit meeting in little more than two years when Putin visited India in December 2004. This was in sharp contrast to the erratic ties India had with Russia while Yeltsin was at the helm. While maintaining a continuity in ensuring a substantive and incremental pattern of relations with the USA and Western Europe, Putin has revived equations with other major Asian nations like China, Japan and India.

In their own ways, both India and Russia are struggling to define their relations with other major players on the global stage in the post- September 11 global context, where the rules of international politics are in a state of flux and where the terms of economic interaction between nations are being reset. Therefore, their continued affirmation of a longstanding friendship assumes more than just a symbolic importance. During Putin's visit to India in December 2002, even as Russia secured India's agreement to intensify the strategic partnership, India was able to receive Russian support for its position on Pakistan, with Russia calling upon Pakistan to end its support for cross-border terrorism (*Putin, in India Asks Pakistanis To End Support for the Militants*). Russia's endorsement of the Indian position on terrorism and Pakistan reflected Russian desires to maintain the traditional goodwill in mutual relations by understanding India's deepest security concerns. This is in sharp contrast to the USA, which has effectively glossed over India's major security concerns with respect to Pakistan-sponsored terrorism in India.

Perhaps the most important element of Indo-Russian bilateral relations is the defence ties between the two countries. Not only is Russia the biggest supplier of defense products to India, but the India–Russia defence relationship also encompasses a wide range of activity, including joint research, design, development, and co-production.[10] Indian and Russian defence companies are not only designing and developing but will also be jointly marketing the anti-ship missile, *Brahmos,* in other countries. Russia has also made a proposal to India to jointly develop a next generation Advanced Jet Trainer with an eye on the global market. Russia has agreed to further expand defecse-supplies ties with India, both in content and range, and has also agreed to give the nod to cooperation in sophisticated spheres of technology, about which the USA and other Western nations have seemed reticent.

Perhaps the most challenging aspect of Indo-Russian relations today is the upgrading of bilateral economic and trade relations, which fails to reflect the potential that exists. In fact, trade between the countries has declined over the last three years. In order to address this problem, Russia has not only been trying to woo Indian investors but has also agreed to use the amount that India owes it as debt from the past to fund joint ventures in the fields of telecommunications, aluminum, and information technology.[11]

However, on various regional and global issues, India and Russia find themselves on the same side. Both have made their position clear with respect to what they see as the unilateral tendencies of US foreign policy, and they would like to see the UN as the proper forum for dealing with issues of international peace and security.[12]

Their geopolitical and security interests in the Central Asian region are also compatible, in so far as religious extremism, terrorism, drug trafficking, smuggling in small arms, and organised crime, emanating largely from Central Asia, threaten both India and Russia equally. The Indo-Russian cooperation seems to be steadily progressing on the basis of the two countries' shared long-term national and geopolitical interests and their common stand on key global and regional problems.

India-China Relations: Mending Fences

Bilateral relations between India and the People's Republic of China have indeed come a long way since their nadir in the immediate aftermath of India's nuclear tests in May 1998. Immediately prior to the nuclear tests, China had been singled out by India's Defence Minister as the 'number one' security threat for India (*India's New Defence Chief Sees Chinese Military Threat*).[13] Following the tests, the Indian Prime Minister wrote to the US President justifying Indian nuclear tests as a response to the threat posed by China. Not surprisingly, China reacted strongly and diplomatic relations between the two countries plummeted to an all-time low.

However, some five years later, relations between the two countries seem to be on the upswing. The visit of the Indian Minister for External Affairs to China in 1999, marked the resumption of high-level dialogue, and the two sides declared that they were not threats to each other. A bilateral security dialogue was also initiated that has helped the two countries to openly express and share their security concerns with each other. India and China also decided to expedite the process of demarcation of the Line of Actual Control (LAC), and the Joint Working Group (JWG) on the boundary question, set up in 1988, has been meeting regularly. As a first step in this direction, the two countries exchanged border maps on the least controversial middle sector of the LAC. The two states are now committed to transforming the 4,056-km LAC into a mutually acceptable and internationally recognised boundary.

The Indian prime minister made a visit to China in June 2003, the first by an Indian premier in a decade. The joint declaration signed during this visit expressed the view that China was not a threat to India. The two states appointed special representatives in order to impart momentum to the border negotiations that have been going on for 22 years, with the Prime Minister's Principal Secretary becoming India's political-level negotiator, replacing the India–China JWG. India acknowledged China's sovereignty over Tibet and pledged not to allow 'anti-China' political activities in India.[14] For its part, China has acknowledged India's 1975 annexation of the former monarchy of Sikkim by agreeing to open a trading post along the border with the former kingdom.

It is at the international level, however, that India and China have found some real convergence of interests. India and China have both expressed concern about the USA's use of military power around the world (Associated Foreign Press, 1999), and both were publicly opposed to the war in Iraq. Both also favour more democratic international economic regimes. They have strongly resisted efforts by the USA and other developed nations to link global trade to labour and environmental standards, realising clearly that this would put them at a huge disadvantage *vis-à-vis* the developed world, thereby hampering their drive towards economic development, the number one priority for both countries.

In recent years, India and China have attempted to build their bilateral relationship on the basis of their larger world-view of international politics. As they have found a distinct convergence of their interests on the world stage, they have used it to strengthen their bilateral relations. However, although India and China share similar concerns about the growing global dominance of the USA, the threat of religious and ethnic movements in the form of terrorism, and the need to accord primacy to economic development, there are a number of obstacles that prevent the Sino-Indian bilateral relationship from achieving its full potential.

India–Russia–China: Prospects of Cooperation in the Twenty–First Century

Prospects of relations between the three countries in the twenty-first century certainly imply coordinate actions taken in response to the challenges of the new century.[15] There is a need to coordinate the actions. Because with the advent of the new century, the international environment in which these three states play the part of sovereign actors has become more intricate and complicated.[16] The commonality of the key national interests and the long-term friendly relations in the field of economy, culture, science and technology create a real possibility for cooperation between three great Eurasian powers. A three-nation cooperation between India, China and Russia has become necessary in the twenty-first century. There are self-evident reasons for this, but the primary rationale is provided by the circumstances in which the three countries find themselves in a world, that has seen so many qualitative changes over the last decade or so.[17] There are advantages of three nation cooperation despite the obvious asymmetries, given the fact that they are amongst the world's largest continental-sized entities and civilisation states. The agenda for future cooperation between china, India and Russia is large. Any discussion or reflection on the prospects and possibilities of cooperation between India, China and Russia began with clear understanding of the wider context in which such cooperation would be possible and would progress.

All three countries have had a long history of interaction, exchange, cooperation and close relationships.[18] In the post-World

War II period, there have been phases of tremendous warmth and dizzying highs among them. There have also been periods of near-total breakdown and actual hostilities (the Sino-Soviet relations in the late sixties and Sino-India relations in the early sixties). It was only in the late seventies that a restructuring of these relationship (particularly India-China and Sino-Soviet relations) begun to be considered afresh. What has become clear to all three was that any such restructuring would be based on a qualitatively different strategic reality that would be shaped by and impinged upon by the weight of history and would in some respects have to virtually start from scratch. There was, for instance, no doubt that there could be no resurrection of any kind of alliance relationship clearly directed against or targeting any third country or any agreement offering unconditional support to the other.[19] The post-cold war scenario heightened the need for restructuring and readjustment and the process was accelerated even more in the mid-nineties in the relationship of all three. Since all three countries support a just and rational new international order with democratisation of international politics and multipolarisation, there are a number of areas possible for their political cooperation in the new century.

Energy Security

One of the major areas of cooperation for the three countries is energy security.[20] Russia is an energy surplus country whereas China and India are energy deficient. If these three states can work together, they can invest in joint projects that could facilitate the flow of oil and gas from Russia into China and India. The axis can improve the overall energy security scenario in Asia and the world. Russian and China struck an unprecedented deal jointly to survey oil and natural gas resources in their border areas. The agreement was signed by officials from China's northeastern province of Heilongjian and the Primorie region of Russia. The new geological survey will focus on three trans–border basins: the Muhe-Ushumun, the Sunwu-Zeysko Bureinskaya and the Sanjiang-Amur. A preliminary survey has reportedly detected an oil and gas field with a maximum reserve of 80 million tons of crude.

ASEAN

All three nations indicated their cooperation with each other for joining ASEAN's Treaty of Amity and Cooperation (TAC) at the Regional Security Forum in Phnom Penh. By doing so Russia, India and China will thus become the first countries outside ASEAN to sign up to the pact in a coordinated demonstration of their desire to forge strategic partnership with ASEAN. They are also keen on strengthening the ASEAN Regional Forum (ARF).[21] China and Russia are also willing to conduct regular discussions on regional security and economic cooperation within the framework of the Asia-Pacific economic cooperation.

UN

In the UN both China and Russia are permanent members of the UN Security Council. And India has been striving for the membership of the UN Security Council. China and Russia understand India's aspiration very well. China is willing to see India play a bigger role in the UN. Russia-China-India subscribe to the principle emphasized in the Millennium Declaration Goal that responsibilities for managing worldwide economic and social development, as well as threats to international peace and security must be shared among the nations of the world and should be exercised multilaterally.[22] These countries also share similar views that as the most universal and representative organisation in the world, the UN must play the central role. All the three nations were disturbed by the Iraq war and protested against what they viewed as a rejection of the rules of the international game. They still back the primacy of the United Nations Security Council in solving crises, and support the principle of non-intervention in internal affairs of other sovereign states. Apart from shared concern of US dominance, the three have other common interest and mutually reinforcing needs.

The US Factor

United States is one of the major factors in the formation of Russia-India-China Axis. As each of the three countries is a major political actor of the world. Relation between Indian-Russian-Chinese community and the United States is one of the most important aspects of the global policy.[23] The turning point was the attack of

11 September 2001, which has triggered the complications and dramatic changes in the whole plethora of international relations. After September 11, there was an intense need to consider the economic aspects of the international security, to formulate the new role of US and these states national interests, to struggle against the international terrorism. India-Russia-China have signaled to the US that its unilaterialism is breeding serious concern among big international players. These are clear manifestations of new trends in Russia-India-China tripartite cooperation and US factor. No doubt all there countries attach importance to their respective relations with US. All of them have indicated that developing relations with the US is not directed against other countries. These three states are opposed to the US hegemony and stressed the need for enhanced cooperation between India, Russia and China to ensure a multi-polar world and a new international political and economic order. The growing US military and diplomatic influence in Central and South Asia is also not in New Delhi's and Moscow's and Beijing's interests. [24]

Globalisation

Comprehensive India-Russia-China cooperation is the suitable option in the present global Scenario. It is true that at present development of the world economy is guided by Western capitalism in contrast to the past. After 11 September 2001, sustained economic development of India, Russia and China has become the engine of global economy. India and China have already entered WTO and Russia is pondering over this issue. There are many similarities in the socio-economic conditions of these three countries. Face to face with economic globalisation, the problems they are encountering also have commonalities. For example, the low–priced goods of transnational companies hit traditional agriculture and Industry. Developed countries are violating regulations and nontariff barriers, draining science and technology personnel and homogenising traditional culture.[25]

The formation of a triangle shows that behind the cooperation there is a great motivation of interest. First, to reduce the damages caused by unreasonable regulations. Second, is to provide an alternative for economic development and third, is to look for a buffer zone in order to avoid economic crisis.[26] All these can become great impetus for trilateral cooperation. Indeed, the goal of trilateral cooperation is for the mutual benefit and most likely will conform to the interest of each country. The prospects of cooperation in product composition, technology, energy, raw material etc., are extremely broad.

Global Terrorism

India-Russia-China have common interests in fighting global terrorism and strengthening politico-economic cooperation in the new historic conditions. Convergence of political and economic interests of these three counties is bringing them closer to each other. If this triangular relationship continues to grow and deepen, it will become a decisive factor in this part of the planet. India-Russia-China during the last decade not only faced the threat of terrorism but also suffered from it. In this way, the three countries are natural geopolitical allies in the struggle against international terrorism and by forming a triangle they can deal better with the menace of terrorism.[27]

Economic and Security Challenges

In terms of their role in total world economic output, India-Russia-China, if taken together, have a weight comparable to that of the European Union. All three nations face great economic and security challenges, which they can solve by cooperating with each other. There is an experience and practice of bilateral cooperation but there is no truly significant trilateral cooperation mechanism yet. At the economic level there is potential for India-Russia and China to cooperate with each other in area such as high technology, machinery, energy, pharmaceuticals, telecommunications, chemicals, etc. Joint ventures could be set up in any of the above-mentioned areas. By coordinating their policies on global economic issues India, Russia and China could drive benefit in the log run.[28]

Maritime Cooperation

A very recent example of the manner in which India-Russia-China cooperation can have an impact on negotiations in multilateral forums was provided by the Maritime Safety Committee meeting of the International Maritime organisation in London.[29] The post-September 11 fears of another surprise incident was the justification for a proposal which seeks voluntary disclosure of all information about a ship that may be anywhere within the radius of 200 nautical miles of a country. At present ships on the high seas do not come under the control of foreign governments unlike airplanes, which fall within the jurisdiction of air traffic control stations on the ground. India, Russia, China and several other countries got together to modify the proposal wanting it to be implemented only by an international agency on a global basis. Sources connected to the Indian delegation that participated in the meeting of the International Maritime Organisation held on March 6 to 8, 2006 at National Maritime Research Institute, Tokyo, Japan Stated that this should not be based on "any unilateral action as it would undermine the force of multilateral organisations".[30] More than anything else, the India-Russia-China trilateral consultation and coordination is meant to offset unilateralism and unipolarity within the global system. It seeks to adhere to consensus building as the main mechanism for decision making within the international system, as this is aptly suited to the existing division of power between the various countries.

Global Warming and the Protection of Ozone Layer

India is a large developing country with nearly 700 million rural population directly depending on climate–sensitive sectors (agriculture, forests and fisheries) and natural resources (such as water, biodiversity, mangroves, coastal zones, grasslands) for their subsistence and livelihoods. Further, the adaptive capacity of dry land framers, forests dwellers, fisher folk, and nomadic shepherds is very low.[31] Climate change is likely to impact all the natural ecosystems as well as socio economic systems as shown by the National Communications Report of India to the UNFCCC.[32] The fourth Assessment Report of the Intergovernmental Panel on Climate Change (IPCC), which emphasized the far-reaching consequences that continued global warming would have across the world, has given fresh impetus to finding solutions to the problem. Therefore, India, China and Russia which are a major energy consumers have been organising a series of meetings to control the global warming and the protection of Ozone Layer.

Human Security

"Human Security" stresses the importance of individual security, and here, the definition of a threat to a person's security is far-reaching. Not only does it include security from war, terrorism and environmental degradation, but tit also encompasses the protection and widening of human rights, protection from inequality and oppression, battling poverty and protection from diseases. The three countries continue expanding and building up a multifaceted, constructive, and increasingly significant partnership dialogue. This cooperation is not directed against any third country, and its supreme objective is to assert the authority of international law, principles of justice, and, first and foremost, principles of peaceful coexistence. The course of current events proves the timeliness and practical value of the great principle of *Panchsheel,* the fiftieth anniversary of which has been celebrated recently in the three countries. These types of mutual-pacts between these three countries would naturally enhance the human security not only in the region but also for the entire mankind.

New Silk Road Policy

As for the nations which the United States tries to make an object of its policy, they, too, are not at all happy to play the offered role. Along with active participation in the SCO, they are putting forward broad initiatives for the system of international relations in the twenty-first century to be polycentric and aimed at economic reforms in a peaceful environment. For example, in the Spring of 1999, Askar Akayev, President of the Republic of Kyrgyzstan, published his manifesto entitled 'Silk Route Diplomacy' which says: "Building of a Nuclear Weapon Free Zone in Central Asia, discontinuing the arms race, and converting defense production, as well as providing proper conditions for sustainable development of all countries along the Great Silk Route without exception – all these would give a reason to hope that in the beginning of the 3rd Millennium, the (silk) Route region, with its enormous potential and resources, would be one of the most prosperous and wealthy in the world; because problems connected with interests of all countries, would be resolved jointly; and all obstacles to free movement of goods, capitals, services and labor in the whole area of the Route would be eliminated. There are sufficient grounds to suggest that all countries of the Great Silk Route would apply maximal efforts to the effect that in the new millennium, only positive impulses of creativity, peace, progress and prosperity would be generated from the region of the Route, which is a vast space crossing the whole mainland of Eurasia from East to West and which unites the rich diversity of cultures, traditions and historic destinies.

This approach is accepted by a number of Asian and European states that are interested in the grand project of the twenty-first century – the Trans–Continental Economic Bridge. In China, for example, this project has been adopted as a government programme. The project means to build a high-tech-based network of high-speed transport and communications lines in the expanses of Eurasia, and thus to unite Asian and European nations in a new type of association for development. The central purpose of such an association would be to build, through joint efforts, an integrated super-modern infrastructure for transport, energy, and communications that would extend from the Pacific through to the Atlantic, and thus provide a basis for rapid economic development of the whole mass of Eurasia in the twenty-first century. As noted in the comprehensive expert assessment of this project, "Having lived though geopolitical manipulations, alienation and conflicts, as well as the Great Game of the colonial powers, peoples of the greatest continent have approached the opportunity to overcome the chronic backwardness of Eurasian inland area with the help of advanced technologies. For the first time in history, Eurasia, as an integrated unit, would arrive at a quite clear economic reality, composed by sovereign states intensively cooperatively with one another."[33]

Coming back to Russia's current strategic partnership with India and China it should be said that an important strategic objective in the central pat of Eurasia is the need to create and to sustain favorable international conditions for successful realisation of planned reforms. This is a point of coincidence among major national interests of India, Russia and China which is multiplied by the existing long traditions of friendly ties in the spheres of economy, culture, science, and technology, Lyndon La Rouche highlighted exactly this point in his presentation of December 3, 2001 in New Delhi, and exactly this point provides a real opportunity for interaction among the three Eurasian giants. However, in practice, the opportunity alone would not be sufficient for such interaction, because the latter could take place only in a certain international environment, which we have to create and for which we shall have to struggle.

In the environment which is taking shape under the influence of other powers, favorable factors work together with quite many unfavorable ones, which could complicate and even frustrate interaction among the three powers, and which are not generated exclusively by bilateral relations within the 'triangle'.[34] So, let us try to systematise the main unfavorable factors, and to weigh the real extent to which such factors could jeopardise attainment of common strategic objectives.

Old and New Aspects of International Security

The first group of factors is connected with international security, as well as its old and new aspects. All strategic threats – or, in the given case, unfavourable factors – are embedded in the changed state of international security. The trends that have generated the change have been accumulated implicitly. The main aspects of the old security structure (in the 1960s–1980s) were represented by the willingness; to avoid nuclear war at the level of the two superpowers; to prevent the growth of local conflicts and wars into a universal holocaust; to block the proliferation of nuclear weapons; to solve the ecological problems of the planet; and, to regulate the demographic explosion.[35]

The disintegration of the Soviet Union activated development of some old tends and generated new ones, such as: (1) So far, the reduction of nuclear weapons and their delivery systems does not guarantee against a nuclear war; (2) The proliferation of nuclear weapons could not be stopped, and now the task is not so much to make such weapons unavailable to states, but rather to individual terrorist organisations and groups; 3) Ecological problems are mounting – both in connection with the U.S. refusal to sign the Kyoto protocol, and in connection with global climate change and the growing number of technology–generated catastrophes ; (4) By all the evidence, demographic problems will be growing until the mid-twenty-first century, which is defined as the final point of demographic transition (i.e., a global self-regulating demographic process); (5) By that time, China's population, for example, would reach the mark of 1.6 billion; (6) The two-pole structure of the would in general and international security in particular, is being replaced by a multi-polar structure of both, which is taking shape in the struggle against the trend towards a U.S. led one-pole world; (7) Hence, there is reason to discuss the United States as playing a new role, of a 'brake' on the development of international relations; (8) in the resolution of international problems, evident attempts are being taken to regard domestic legislation as higher than the UN Charter; (9) The creation of the EU and the role of united Europe carry both positive and negative potentials of the new system of international relations; (10) India and China have appeared in the position of major world powers, and their ole will be growing; (11) As proved by the financial crisis of 1997-98, the economic security of nations is no less important than security in the military and political spheres; (12) The role of such a factor of world development as the Islamic Revolution is growing rapidly; and (13) Finally, factors have appeared such as international terrorism, the international drug business, corruption and crime in many spheres of human activity, etc., all of which serve as a reason to discuss the process of criminal globalisation. The above list of factors could be crowned by the appearance of a worldwide anti-globalist movement.[36]

The second group of factors is connected with a struggle within the United Nations and for the United Nations. The UN was established as a collective guarantor of international security. Nowadays, we hear the widely disseminated view that the UN is somehow outdated and lagging behind rapidly developing international relations. To some extent, this view seems correct, especially in the context of several substantial failures of the UN in the last several years. The failures include; the Yugoslavian crisis of 1999, when NATO was placed over the UN; the year 2001, announced by the UN as the Year of Dialogue Among Civilisations, and "creamed"[37] by the events of September 11 in the United States; and, the resolution by the U.S. Congress allowing the U.S. President to attack Iraq at his own discretion, neglected the UN resolutions and inspections. Today, if one asks the question as to "Who is interested in the UN?" the answer will be; "Nobody but, probably, Taiwan, who wants to be back in there." However, to bury the UN would be premature.[38]

Along with the ever more frequent neglect of the UN on the part of the United States and NATO, several objective factors, too, are responsible for weakening the UN's role. First, apart from the five leading countries – being the UN founders and permanent members of its Security Council – a group of other important actors has appeared on the world scene, and hence in the UN. These countries – India, Japan, Brazil, Germany, and Canada – seek to strengthen their positions in the United Nations. Reorganisation of the UN structure has been on the agenda for several years already, but so far, consensus on this issue seems to be quite distant from now. Second, there are a number of new multinational associations (European Union) and international organisations – both regional (for example, APEC) and specialised (OPEC, WTO), Regular summit and ministerial meetings within the framework of such organisations somehow dissolve the need to delegate a number of problems to the UN. At the same time, informal but regular summits of the G-8 or Asia–Europe also remove many issues from the UN agenda.

It appears that along with reorganisation of the UN structure, the authority of this organisation as the only world–scale forum to address the problems of international security could be enhanced by such measures, as; to conduct the G-8 summit at the UN – while resolving global issues, the G-8 must not isolate itself from the rest of the world, because otherwise it would place itself in confrontation with many states and with many movements; to continue the Year of Dialogue Among Civilisations and, to this end, to select the UN as the venue for the Asia–Europe summit, Islamic Conference Summit and Conference on Islam and Europe (the latter planned to take place in Spain); to conduct the APEC and OPEC summits within the framework of the UN; to hold a special session of the UN General Assembly that would address unification of all forces in the struggle against international terrorism. The UN could make all the above listed summits more transparent for the world public, and thus create an atmosphere of better confidence in the world. Such Eurasian powers as India,

Russia and China are interested, probably more than others, in the UN being again an efficient instrument of peace for the world community, and this is one of their shared positions where they have started to apply coordinated efforts.[39]

The third group of unfavorable factors is connected with the economic aspects of international security. In the new system of international relations at the dawn of this century, the economic component has grown considerably. This growth has been predetermined by three elements: (1) the objective course of globalisation; (2) depletion of world energy resources; and (3) global ecology problems – such as the shortage of freshwater and depletion of soils. Apart from these rather obvious factors, there are factors, which are not very visible for the broad public, but which could blow up all economic ties in the world.

The situation is presented most fully and clearly in the Resolution of September 25, 2002, passed by the Italian National Parliament, with regard to authorising the government to take measures that would help Argentina to overcome the crisis. The Parliament proceeded from recognition of the fact that escalation of the banking and financial crisis, which started from crises of 1997 in Asia, Russia and Latin America, and has lasted through to the recent failure of the new economy in the United States, the massive and, so far, lasting banking collapse in Japan, and the bankruptcy of Argentina, cannot but cause concern in all countries—among the population, ruling classes, companies, investors, and depositors – because this is not some chance string of events, but rather expresses the crisis of the entire (global) financial system, marked by the staggering gap between the volume of speculative capital – worth $400 trillion ($140 trillion of which the United States accounts for) – and a world gross product worth only $40 trillion. Such preparations seem to be a reasonable element of interaction among India, Russia and China within the framework of their constructive partnership. The prospects for interaction in the twenty-first century among such countries as Russia, China, others SCO members countries, and India, Mongolia, Iran – i.e., the countries that historically are connected with the center of Eurasia—are not at all exhausted by the vectors addressed in this presentation. Certainly, interaction of all these countries must be put on the solid platform of economic and science–technology cooperation.[40]

Problems or Drawbacks of the Strategic Alliance

The India-Russia-China relationship issue has been overblown out of proportion ever since it cropped up as an idea in 1999. The so-called 'triangle' has been very disappointing so far. This fact needs to be recognised. The main message of this presentation being that this legendary triangle needs a strong infusion of business commonsense.[41] The word 'strategic', which has many meanings, is used less frequently these days while defining India-Russia-China relationship. It is also another matter that all three sides are accusing one another of dragging their feet for the lethargic pace at which this relationship is evolving. Former Russian PM, Yevgeny Primakov, had proposed a India – Russia – China strategic triangle in 1999. The war in Kosovo, in the heart of Europe, had rattled the continent and Primakov was acting as a diplomatic combatant in defending Russian interests. He floated this idea in this backdrop. He clearly had an anti-US intention for formulating this India-Russia-China alliance idea.[42] None of these countries will antagonise the US to provide a fillip to this relationship. Maintaining their respective relationship with the US is top priority for all three countries.

New Delhi and Beijing were not inspired with the perspective of the trilateral strategic partnership because of the abovementioned reason. The two countries are not ready to challenge Washington just because of the fact that they are happy with their cooperation with the USA in comparison with Primakov's idea to come into a certain political alliance with Russia. In addition, the US administration has recently lifted restrictions for arms deliveries to India, which might cause very big problems to the Russian defense export to this country. The USA does not have an intention to make such a concession to China, though. A chief constraint for the triangular alliance is India's burgeoning relations with the United States. Since September 2004, as part of the new strategic framework between the US and India, the two countries have drifted toward expanded cooperation on an array of military and security issues. The US offered India new defence and security incentives including advanced fighter aircraft and US–made theatre missile defences.[43] The Indo-US relations took new heights when, on 28 June 2005, the two countries signed the New Framework for US–India

Defence Relations (NFDR). The NFDR vowed for bilateral relations for the next 10 years on various levels, which included joint weapons production, cooperation on missile defence and the transfer of technology.[44] If opposition to the US had been the prime factor of the emergence of this triangle, the Indo-US agreement has substantially diluted the spirit of this move.

In addition, the USA is an extremely important trade partner for India and China. Russia will not be able to make a competition at this point, at least in the nearest perspective. Needless to mention that neither Delhi nor Beijing will agree to sacrifice the profit for the sake of a rather obscure goal. To crown it all, both India and China used to experience keen rivalries in the struggle for their influence in the Asian region. Pakistan was supporting China in that struggle, whereas India was having traditional problems with it.

The clarity in the relationship reduces or gets muddled when the main problem is sought to be tackled and that is economic issues. Although, a number of initiatives are under way in bilateral networks between the countries, but a viable platform for all three countries for business has to be approached with renewed vigour by the concerned diplomats. The issue becomes tricky when one looks at geo-strategic issues. Carving Russia's 'oil cake' is one such issue. Here, India and China are competitors. Coordination for pipeline routes is also a subject for further discussions.

According to pessimistic school of thought, one of the main challenges to the triangle lies in its basic structure. India and China, at the opposite ends of the base of this triangle, have to forge strong relationships and to overcome the mistrust prevailing over decades.[45] Despite improvement in Sino-Indian relations their historical baggage still blocks their relations. The border dispute remains unresolved.

Though areas of trilateral cooperation may be somewhat limited, important areas of bilateral cooperation do exist. The most important being 'energy'. On this issue, however, Russian policy seems somewhat difficult to understand. While Russia is seen as Saudi Arabia in Europe, it supplies gas and oil to Europe without hard bargaining on technology transfers and bargaining only on cost and pricing. The policy towards India and China is very different. Looking at the issue from the Indian or the Chinese perspective, why should technology transfers become a bargaining point when they are not an issue when discussing oil/gas supplies with the EU? This is an issue that needs to be addressed. Russian aspirations of developing its technology industry are well understood but, Russian policy must also take into account the energy needs of its partners.[46]

On its part India should pursue the idea of trilateral vigour for three reasons. One such cooperation would provide India space for manoeuvreability in its negotiations with the west. It would also bring about greater balance in its policy. Secondly, from the perspective of its deep geopolitical and security interests in the region (Central Asia), trilateral cooperation holds enhanced significance. The level of activity in the Central Asian region has intensified. On the one hand is the military presence of the West and on the other hand Russia is making serious attempts to build new security structures in the region. The Shanghai Cooperation Organisation has been institutionalised and President Putin hopes to create a Collective Security Treaty Organisation. How these two organisations will shape up and how effective an instrument they will emerge is difficult to say at this juncture, but India could be left out from an area that is of vital importance to it. Thirdly, the role of Asia is growing in international politics and as one of the major Asian countries India could drive benefits by cooperating with other major Asian countries. From this perspective India should make serious efforts to see that trilateral cooperation moves forward.[47]

V. Conclusion

It is important to realise that in the context of the economic situation prevailing in India, Russia and China all of whom have to give primacy to eradicating poverty and unemployment, development is the essential foundation, which is needed for ensuring the implementation of democratisation and human rights. Maintaining social peace and providing a regime of public law and good governance are necessary preconditions for promoting development. Trilateral cooperation between India, Russia and China will enable them to minimise expenditure on security, solve any disputes through negotiations and promote trade, communications, telelinks, tourism, cultural and educational exchanges and development of technology, good administrative, political and fiscal governance as well as literacy and social modernisation. A multipolar world order of which this trilateral cooperation will be an essential dimension and will reinforce it would promote a beneficial globalisation and the prospects of a peaceful world in the twenty first century. It is noteworthy that the leading countries of the Shanghai Cooperation Organisation – India, Russia and China are also for the first time invitees to the G-8 meeting. This only demonstrates that the multipolar world is itself a part of the globalisation process and is creating a more balanced distribution of power as well as a system of checks and balances in which the greater the economic development and social awareness the greater are the prospects of democratisation.

On the same occasion, it would be an exaggeration to believe that the establishment of tripartite India-Russia-China cooperation and their successful breakthrough into the future will be flawless and smooth in the present scenario. A lot of difficulties and obstacles are in store for them, which could be overcome as far as the cooperation is defined by objective circumstances and by positive initiation of the leaders of these three countries.

References

1. Kuchins, Andrew C. "Russia's relations with China and India: Strategic partnerships", *'yes; strategic alliances, no'*, Demokratizatsiya, Spring 2001, p.1.
2. Ibid., p.2.
3. T.T. Poulose, "Russia-China-India A Strategic Triangle", *South Asian Studies,* Paper no. 1424, 21.06.2005. p.7.
4. Waltz, K., Structural Realism After the Cold War, *International Security,* 25.1.2000, pp. 28-42.
5. Reuters, China Russia to Strengthen Anti US Coalition, 18 November 1998. p.38.
6. Ibid.
7. Ibid.
8. Nemets A.V., Scherer J., The Emerging Sino- Russian Axis, *The World & I* 15 (6) : 61-75, 2000.

9. Shukla V., Russia in south Asia: A view from India, in Chufrin G. (ed.,) *Russia and Asia: the Emerging Security Agenda,* Stockholm: SIPRI, 1999, pp. 34-59.
10. Dixit J.N., Moscow Reaches Out, *Indian Express,* 12 December 2002.
11. Cheria, J. A Strategic Parntership, " Frontline" 14-27 October 2000. pp. 52- 59.
12. Ibid., p.59.
13. Nirmala Joshi, Possibility for India-Russia-China's Trilateral Cooperation, in *India-Russia Future Strategic Trends,* Eds. V.D. Chopra, p.187.
14. Benwang, Preliminary Analysis of Main Features of China's New Security Concepts, *Foreign Affairs Journal,* Beijing No. 665, September, 2002, p.37.
15. Vinod C. Khanna, Strengthening the Role of UN and China-India-Russia Cooperation in UN Related Issues, *China Report 39:3, 203,* New Delhi, pp. 385-386.
16. Ibid., p.386.
17. Ibid.
18. R.L. Bhatia has argued on the Triangle formation in his article on Indo-Russia, Sino-Russia, Sino-India Triangle in *Indo-Russia Future Strategic Trends,* Eds. V.D. Chopra, pp.29-35.
19. Ibid.
20. Nirmala Joshi, op. cit., pp.188.
21. Leonid Ivashov, Russian General Comments on Topical Geo-Political Issues, No.7, *Daily Review,* Moscow, January 2000.
22. *Asian Age,* 7 November 2001.
23. Xu Jain and Guo Zhenyuan, *Major Threats and Dangers facing China,* FBIS – CHI, 2003 – 0730.
24. Ibid.
25. V.D. Chopra, India-Russia-China: Changing Equation in *India-Russia Future Strategic Trends,* pp. 187-195.
26. Ibid., p.195.
27. Report on Bilateral Relations between India and Russian Federation, Ministry of External affairs, Central and East European Division, 28 November 2002.
28. *Russian National Security Doctrine,* January 10, 2000, CDSP Vol.52, No.4. pp.19-20.
29. Russian Foreign Minister Promotes Strategic Triangle, *South Asian Tribune,* Issue No. 21, December 16-22, 2002.
30. Ibid.

31. Nivedita Das Kundu, *Russia-India-China: Prospects for Trilateral Cooperation*, Institute for Defence Studies and Analysis, New Delhi, 2005, p.24.
32. Ibid., p.25.
33. Peoples Daily Novsoti, in http://www.pegmusic.com/news-rci.html Dec 2, 2002.
34. Report on "India, China and Russia Team up Against High Seas Policing", *The Economic Times*, 8/6/2005 p.1.
35. Ibid., p.2.
36. Ibid.
37. Ravindranath N.H. and Sathaye, J., *Climate Change and Developing Countries*, Kluwer Academic Publishers, Dordrecht, Netherlands, 2002, p.16.
38. Ibid., p.17.
39. *India's Initial National Communications to the United Nations Framework Convention on Climate Change*, Ministry of Environment and Forests, New Delhi -2004.
40. A. Akayev, Diplomatiya Shelkovogo Puti (Silk Route Diplomacy) (Bishkek: 1999), pp.1-3.
41. V.S. Myasnikov, " Kontinentalnyi most-proyekt XXI Veka" (Continental Bridge: Project of the 21st Century), Metally Evrazii, natsionalnoye obozreniye, 1997, No. 3, p.8.
42. Ibid.
43. Ilan Berman, "Trilateral Alliance: Russia, China and India may be on a collision course with the US", *National Review*, 5 May 2005, p.11.
44. Ibid.
45. *Washington Times* (Washington), 29 June 2005.
46. Subhash Kapila, "China –India Strategic Alliance: should not be Unthinkable" http://www.saag.org/%5Cpapers14%Caper 1375.html (accessed on 24 August 2005.)
47. Nirmala Joshi, "India-Russia-China-Prospects for Trilateral Cooperation", in V.D. Chopra (Ed), *New Trends in Indo-Russian Relations*, Kalpaz Publication, New Delhi, 2003, p.191.

7

Conclusion

In the changing dynamics of international politics set in motion by the end of the cold war and the break-up of the Soviet Union in 1991, there were paradigm shifts in the nature of relations among countries. India and the Russian Federation, however, were soon able to find a new basis for reestablishing their close and friendly relations. Within a span of a decade, Indo-Russian relations have evolved into a strategic partnership. This implies a qualitative higher level of relationship reflecting mutual trust and confidence. Generally, it has been observed that whenever the geopolitical and strategic interests of two countries coincide, the ensuing relationship between them is often warm, close and friendly

After the breakup of the Soviet Union, there was uncertainty about the future of India's relations with the Russian Federation. Indian concern was whether the special relations it enjoyed would undergo a change or not. Immediately after the breakup of the Soviet Union, there was a debate even in Russia about its future policy towards South Asia. There was a view that Russian policy should be equidistant, in which both India and Pakistan enjoyed the same emphasis. Hence, in the early years, Russian policy towards India was one of benign neglect. This phase soon gave way, and in January 1993, during President Yeltsin's visit to India, the earlier treaty was replaced by a new one: The Treaty of Friendship and Cooperation. However, it was with Prime Minister Narasimha Rao's visit to Russia in June 1994 that Indo-Russian ties were put on a firm foundation. "The Moscow Declaration on the Protection of Interests of Pluralist States" signed by India and Russia has become the bedrock of the relations. The Declaration drew attention not only to the nature of the challenges faced by the two countries, but also focused attention on the source from which this threat emanated for both. It also reiterated support of the signatories for each other's territorial integrity. This is highly important given the fact that India and Russia were battling with these challenges in Kashmir and Chechnya, respectively. In the changed context, it was the space that lay between India and Russia that acquired significance. Once again, it was the commonality of their geopolitical interests that paved the way for the relationship to become strong and stable.

Later, India and Russia backed opposition to the Taliban that had crystallised into the Northern Alliance. On the issue of religious extremism and terrorism, India and Russia share many commonalities: the source of tension, funding, training, etc. India and Russia wanted a secular Central Asia working towards a democratic setup. From this perspective, stability and security were important. Instability hampers growth and helps in sustaining extremism and terrorism to an extent. Consequently, India and Russia have established institutional linkages to strengthen this aspect. To date, this commonality has not diminished. Russia views India as a major regional power whose involvement in international politics would make a positive contribution.

Among the other initiatives taken by Russia is the idea of an India-Russia-China strategic triangle, coming together in the interests of the challenges faced by them in the region. During Primakov's visit to India in December 1998, he proposed at an informal level that India-Russia- China should come together and form a strategic triangle in the interests of peace and stability in the region. The initial response of India was one of caution that could be explained by the fact that a strategic triangle implied common perceptions and convergence of interests *vis-à-vis* a common threat. Similarly, China expressed no opinion on this idea. One of the impacts of the events of 9/11 has been that China has developed a positive attitude towards the idea of trilateral cooperation. Possibly, the renewal of Pakistani-American cooperation could have had an impact on Chinese strategic thinking. It was perhaps with the idea of furthering the cause of trilateral cooperation that President Vladimir Putin embarked on his Asian tour by visiting China and later India in December 2002.

In a TV interview, Primakov said, "It is shared interest in maintaining security and stability in Central Asia and Afghanistan that may give flesh and blood to the idea of a Moscow-Beijing-Delhi triangle." The foreign ministers of the three countries have been meeting on the sidelines of the UN General Assembly to discuss issues of common concern at the global and regional level. Issues such as energy security, trade and enhancing contacts have been discussed. In May 2005, the foreign ministers of the three countries had their first full-fledged meeting.

At the political level, both India and Russia have steadfastly supported each other on issues of crucial importance. Russia's position on the Kashmir issue is very close to India's position. Taking note of President Pervez Musharraf's speech of January 12, 2002, a joint statement issued at the end of Foreign Minister Igor Ivanov's visit to India (February 3–4, 2002) said, "Pakistan's commitment can only be judged by the concrete action Pakistan takes on ground." In other words, Russia showed complete understanding of India's position on cross-border terrorism and its reluctance to engage in a dialogue with Pakistan at that time, while on the Chechen issue, India expressed support for the steps taken by Russia to protect its territorial integrity and constitutional order in the rebellious Chechen Republic. On the question of terrorism and the need to initiate countermeasures, India and Russia had similar views. At an international forum, India and Russia have vigorously championed the need to combat this menace with a greater sense of urgency. The two countries have often reiterated their deep commitment to fighting religious extremism and terrorism. Several institutional linkages have been established to facilitate exchange and sharing of information and advancing the common interests in the best possible way.

The congruence of views between India and Russia had a favourable impact on defense cooperation. This cooperation was put on a firm footing with the landmark Sukhoi deal signed in late 1996. The salutary features of Indo-Russian defence cooperation were its long-term-basis transfer of technology, modernisation of existing equipment, and access to the latest equipment, weaponry, etc. in the Russian arsenal. In fact, defense cooperation had gone beyond the main "buyer-seller" syndrome and had moved to the plane of joint design, research and production. Recently, the chief of the Indian Armed Forces was in Russia to assure the Russians that enhanced interaction with the United States would not lead to a drift towards that country on the question of defence cooperation. Even on the nuclear issue, Russia showed considerable understanding of the Indian position when the Pokhran-II blasts took place in 1998. Initially, there was disquiet in Russia over the blasts, but later, Russia did not go public in criticising India. Importantly, it did not impose sanctions. In fact, in June 1998, an agreement for the construction of two 1000-MW reactors at Kundankulam was signed during the visit of the Russian Minister for Atomic Energy, Evgenii Adamov.

It can be said with some degree of certainty that Indo-Russian ties will not witness any drastic fluctuations. As long as core interests continue to coincide, such a possibility is ruled out. Moreover, there is no direct clash of interests to anticipate such an eventuality. The above-mentioned new areas of cooperation would further strengthen the relationship. Above all, however, political will is required. But, times change, and so do policies and priorities of nations. Even though the defence-technical cooperation between the two countries has been growing at a rapid pace, trade and economic ties are lagging woefully behind, despite the plethora of agreements initiated and the optimism exuded by their leadership. What is the mutual interest that sustains the India-Russia relationship today? A strategic partnership cannot survive on nostalgia; it needs substance. The relationship survives and thrives because both Russia and India see the other as relevant to their respective national priorities. Both recognise that, as rising powers likely to play an increasingly larger role on the world stage in the coming decades, there is mutual gain in strengthening the edifice of a deep-rooted partnership that has survived the turbulence of the nineties. There is a shared interest in weakening US global hegemony and in creating a multipolar world. There is reciprocal support and understanding for each other's interests and policies in their respective strategic neighbourhoods – South Asia in the case of India, and the former Soviet Union in the case of Russia. There is a complementarity of interests in important fields of cooperation such as oil and gas, defence, nuclear, space, science and technology— all areas that constitute Russia's core strength and globally competitiveness and, reciprocally, areas where India needs foreign assistance and collaboration.

In the context of a perspective for the future, a holistic view ought to be taken of the many areas of cooperation between India and Russia. Even within the realm of military cooperation, it is imperative for upgrading the military-technical cooperation to a much broader 'Defence Cooperation' at a strategic level. This argument arises from two major aspects of the bilateral relationship that is indisputable. Firstly, relations between India and Russia have stood the test of time. They have come out stronger after negotiating many a challenge. Second, particularly after the Treaty of Peace and Friendship of 1971, Russia has increasingly treated India as an important strategic partner. As the much touted 'new world order' is evolving, many developments warrant that both countries should chart a broader course in our bilateral relations. A few global, regional and strategic issues that warrant such reorientation on the part of India's thinking are highlighted in succeeding paragraphs to illustrated this issue as follows.

As stated earlier, Russia and India have pledged to cooperate in the joint development of aircraft, ships, submarines and space-based navigational systems. While these are indeed welcome developments and will further consolidate military-technical cooperation, it is important that future requirements of weapon systems and platforms must be derived from respective doctrines. In the case of Indo-Russian military cooperation, dealing with common threats to peace and stability within the region in particular and the world in general offer good common ground for development of doctrines.

After doctrines for specific threats are developed with rigorous debate and scrutiny, the scientific and financial investment in the development of systems would be justified and, in due course, stand validated. One such area of common threat perception is counter-terrorist and counter-insurgency operations. Such an effort in no way would encroach upon the sovereign right of both our nations to develop our respective security architectures and strategies.

Terrorism is now recognised as a major threat to peace and security; its dimension is global while its manifestation may differ in different parts of the world. It is in fact a new form of warfare that is adopted by hostile forces that recognise no international boundaries or laws. Russia and India have unequivocally condemned terrorism and have resolved to consolidate joint efforts in suppressing financing of international terrorism and fighting illicit drug trafficking. There are many other important facets of countering terrorism such as sharing of intelligence and experience to develop techniques and concepts. Technology could also assist security forces engaged in fighting terrorist organisations; anti-IED (improvised explosive device) systems is a case in point. This needs to be encapsulated in a comprehensive and well-articulated counter-terrorism doctrine. Both countries should expand the military technical cooperation further to include preparation of conceptual framework for such a doctrine. Insurgency is yet another area of concern. Like terrorism, its conduct differs from region to region. Both countries should share their respective experiences in counter-insurgency operations to assist the respective security forces to improve methods, tactics and techniques in dealing with the problem.

Space and cyber space are the new frontiers of national security. India and Russia have been cooperating with each other in the field of space technologies for many years. India is opposed to weaponisation of space; our space programme is designed for developmental requirements. Some of India's satellites perform meteorological functions considered very important for the agricultural sector that is a major component of our economy. If such satellites are threatened with destruction, it will affect food production and, India's food security. There would be other similar concerns both for Russia and India. It is, therefore, axiomatic that both countries need to go beyond the current project like Glonass and identify areas that could be considered potentially destabilising to common security and peace in the region.

Information technology has become an important aspect in almost every field of human activity. Cyber security has consequently become vital ingredient of the security environment. This aspect also received attention during the visit of President Putin to New Delhi in January2007. Once again it is necessary to explore specific areas for military-technical cooperation in this field. However, in order to give a sound foundation and impart long-term stability to Indo-Russian relations, trade and economic cooperation, which is currently at a worryingly low level, has to increase and diversify. This is the most challenging task before the two leaders, because in both countries this is now a private sector driven activity. Governments can nudge and persuade, but cannot compel or direct business. One persistent and fundamental problem that has defied solution is the enormous difficulty that Indian businessmen face in getting visas for Russia. One can expect progress on all these sectors during President Putin's visit. Of course, there will be tough negotiations and no "friendship" prices. Bureaucratic indifference and rigidities on both sides also constitute formidable hurdles that will have to be overcome. But it is evident that both countries will make special efforts to bring back the vigor and dynamism in the relationship that has been missing for some time.

Finally, India needs to guard against possible uncertainties in a post-Putin era when India may have to deal with a new generation of Russian leaders who are not so familiar with India. It is heartening therefore that Putin's last official visit to India is such a high-profile one. This valuable exercise in public diplomacy, which will continue through the "Year of Russia" in India next year and the "Year of India" in Russia in 2009, will make an important contribution in creating better appreciation, particularly among the increasingly influential younger generation in both Russia and India, of the importance of the India-Russia relations in the foreign policy and overall national interests of both countries. It will undoubtedly generate the much-needed wider public interest, support and understanding in both countries that will serve to provide greater depth and long-term stability to this exceedingly important and mutually beneficial strategic partnership that has stood the test of time.

Therefore, one can say that Russia and India have enjoyed a close strategic partnership for over a quarter of century. One could say that this was a logical corollary to India's strategic setting in the cold war period. And, now that the cold war is long over, there are bound to be changes in this relationship. India itself has moved out of the shadow of Russia and striking a new strategic partnership with the United States. Similarly, Russia has been moving towards a closer strategic relationship with China. Notwithstanding the above, what cannot be ignored is that both Russia and India for different reasons need to continue with keeping alive their strategic partnership. India has a predominant dependence on Russia for its military hardware requirements, particularly for its Navy and Air Force. This even in normal course, linking it to shelf-life of existing Russian-origin military inventories could extend to another 25-30 years. India would be well advised not to put all its eggs in one basket (USA) and continue with a good proportion of Russian military hardware.

Besides the political connotation of such a step, it could provide the basis for a more economical option of joint R&D and production of military hardware. Russia, on the other had needs to invest more heavily in the health of a sound Indo-Russian strategic partnership. It has to revise its attitudinal approaches. India is no longer a junior partner in this relationship but emerging as a virtual co-equal.

Since the military component is the most vital ingredient of the Indo-Russian strategic partnership, Russia would be well advised not to allow commercial approaches to dominate Indo-Russian defence deals, but adopt politico-military approaches to nurture the relationship. In other words, under changing circumstances, both India and Russia have to re-invent their strategic partnership, keeping uppermost in their minds that the value of the Indo-Russian strategic partnership has not been devalued.

Bibliography

Adhikar, G., Ed., *Documents of the History of the Communist Pary of India,* I, New Delhi, 1971.

Appadorai, A., and Arora, V.K., *India in World Affairs 1957-58,* New Delhi, Stering, 1975.

Aslund, Anders, "How small is the Soviet National Income?" in Henry S. Rowen and Charles Wolf, Jr., eds., *The Impoverished Superpower: Perestroika and the Soviet Military Burden,* San Francisco: Institute for Contemporary Studies, 1990.

Ayoob, Mohammed and Subrahmanyam, K., *The Liberation War,* New Delhi, 1972.

Bakshi, Jyotsna, advanced her argument on Russia's Post-Pokhran Dilemma, *Strategic Analysis,* August 1998.

Balabushevich, V.V. and Prasad, Bimla, eds., *India and the Soviet Union: A Symposium,* New Delhi, 1969.

Bhabani, Sengupta, *Fulcrum of Asia, Relations among China, India, Pakistan and USSR,* New York, 1970.

Bhatia Vinod, *Indo-Soviet Relations: Problems and Prospects,* Panchsheel Publishers, New Delhi, 1991.

Bhatia, R.L. has argued on the Triangle formation in his article on Indo-Russia, Sino-Russia, Sino-India Triangle in *Indo-Russia Future Strategic Trends,* Eds. V.D. Chopra, pp. 29-35.

Bhatia, Vinod, *Jawaharlal Nehru and the Making of Indo-Soviet Relations 1917-47,* Panchsheel Publishers, Delhi, 1981.

Brown, A., and M. Kaser, *Soviet Policies for the 1980s* Oxford, 1982.

Budhraj, V.S., *Soviet Russia and the Hindustan Sub-continent,* Bombay, 1973.

Bulganin, N.A. and Khrushchev, N.S., *Visit of Friendship to India, Gurma and Afghanistan: Speeches and official Documents,* November – December 1955, Moscow, 1956.

Chengxu, Yang, The Possiblity and Prospects for Developing Russia-India-China Relations, in *China Report*38:1 2002, Sage Publications, New Delhi, Thousand Oaks, London, pp95-100.

Chenoy, Anuradha M., *Making of New Russia,* New Delhi, Har-Anand Publishers, 2001.

______________, "Soviet New Thinking on National Liberation Movements: Continuity and Changes", Roger Kanet and Debrah Miner ed., *Soviet Foreign Policy in Transition,* Cambridge: Cambridge University Press, 1992.

Chopra, Pran., *Before and After the Indo-Soviet Treaty,* New Delhi, 1982.

Chopra, V.D., *India and the Socialist World,* Allied, New Delhi, 1983.

______________ "Indo – Russian Relations: Prospects, Problems and Russia Today" Kalpaz publications, New Delhi, 2001.

______________, *New Trends in Indo-Russian Relations,* Gyan Books, New Delhi, 2003.

Conley, Jerome M., 'India-Russia Military and Nuclear Cooperation: Implications for US Security.' US Air Force, *National Strategic Institute Studies Paper,* February 2000.

______________ "Indo-Russian Military and Nuclear Cooperation: Implications for U.S. Security Interests" *INSS Occasional Paper 31, Proliferation Series,* February 2000.

Dash, P.L., 'Soviet Disintegration and Challengers in Indo-CIS Relations' in Stephen P Cohen, Ed. *South Asia After the Cold War: International Perspectives:* ACDIS Papers, New Delhi, 1992.

Degras, Jane, ed., *Soviet Documents on Foreign Policy,* I, London, 1951. *Foreign Poicy of India: Text of Document 1947-59,* Lok Sabha Secretariat, New Delhi, 1959; 2nd ed.

Dixit, J. N., *Across Borders: Fifty Years of India's Foreign Policy,* New Delhi, Picus Books, 1998.

Gaikwad Sanjay, *Dynamics of Indo-Soviet Relations: The Era of Indira Gandhi,* Deep and Deep Publications, New Delhi, 1990.

Ghatate, N.M., ed., *Indo–Soviet Treaty; Reactions and Reflections,* New Delhi, 1972.

Gidadhubli, R.G. "Decade of Foreign Policy: Russia's Struggle for Big Power Status", Monograph, Centre for Studies on Indochina & South Pacific, Sri Venkateshwara University, Tirupati, 2002.

_____________, "Russian Economy in Transition and Its Implications on India-Russia Economic Relations," Monograph, Centre for Studies on Indochina & South Pacific, Sri Venkateshwara University, Tirupati, 2002.

Gogoi, Biplob, "Military-Technical collaboration between India and Russia: An Overview of the Post-Soviet Period", *India Quarterly,* 58 (3-4), July-December 466 *Strategic Analysis*/Apr-Jun 2006 2002, p. 307.

Grover, Verinder, *International Relations and Foreign Policy of India,* Vol. 6 and 7, Deep & Deep Publications, Rajouri Garden, New Delhi, 1992.

Gupta, Sisir., India and Soviet Union, *Current History,* March 1963.

Hemen, Roy, *Indo-Soviet Relations, 1955-71,* Bombay, Jaico Publishing House, 1973.

Imama, Zafar, "Effects of Russian Revolution in India," *St. Authony's Papers,* No. 18, London, 1966.

Ivashov, Leonid, Russian General Comments on Topical Geo-Political Issues, No.7, *Daily Review,* Moscow, January 2000.

Jain, Girilal, "Indo-Soviet Relations", *The Institute of Defence Studies and Analyses Journal* 2 (1), 1969.

Jayashekar, *Leading Sectors in Soviet Economic Development,* National Publishing House, New Delhi, 1983.

_____________, *A Review of Rupee Trade Booklet* published by Forum of Free Enterprise, Bombay, 1983.

Joshi, Nirmala M., "*India and Russia: Historical Linkages in the Twentieth Century*", presented in the International Conference on Three Millennia of Contacts between India, Russia and Central Asia, Organised 35 by the ICHR, New Delhi, 6-8 November, 2001.

Kapur, Harish, *The Soviet Union and the Emerging Nations: A Case Study of Soviet Policy towards India,* London, 1972.

Kapur, K.P., *Soviet Strategy in South Asia,* New Delhi, 1983.

Katragadda, G., "Indo-Soviet Trade Exceeds Targets", *ISCUS Bulletin,* Vol, V, No. 1 January 1972.

_____________ "Soviet Contribution to India's Defence", *Indo– Soviet Co-operation,* New Delhi, 1971.

_____________, *Soviet Relations with India and Pakistan,* New Delhi, 1971.

Kaushik, Devendra, *Soviet Contribution to India's Defence: Indo-Soviet Co-operation,* New Delhi, 1971.

______________, *The Indian Ocean – A Strategic Dimension,* Vikas Publishing House, Delhi, 1983.

Kemp, P.M., *Bharat-Rus: An Introduction to Indo-Russian Contacts and Traves from Medival Times to the October Revolution,* New Delhi, 1958.

Khan, Rasheeduddin, Ed., *India and the Soviet Union,* Delhi, Allied Publishers, 1975.

Khanna, Vinod C., Strengthening the Role of UN and China-India-Russia Cooperation in UN Related Issues, *China Report* 39:3,203, New Delhi, pp385-386.

Kodikara, Shelton U., 'South Asian Security Dilemmas in the Post-Cold War World' in Stephen P Cohen, Ed, *ACDIS Papers,* New Delhi 1992.

Komarov, E.N., *Indo-Soviet Cooperation: Historical Background and Present-day Development,* Allied, Bombay, 1976.

Kulkarni, Maya, *Indo–Soviet Political Relations Since Bandung Conference* 1955, Bombay, 1968.

Kundu, Nivedita Das, on "Indo-Russian Relations: An Overview", available at http://www.helsinki.fi/aleksanteri/english/publications/ap_das_ kundu.htm, Also See Jasjit Singh, Trends in Defence Expenditure, *Asian Strategic Review* 1998-99.

Lounev, Russia and India Political Cooperation in the Sphere of Global, Regional and Bilateral Relations, *China Report* 381, 2002.

Mahapatra Debidatta, Aurobinda, *India-Russia Partnership: Kashmir, Chechnya and Issues of Convergence,* New Century Publications, New Delhi, 2006.

Mandelbaum, Michael, Ed., *The New Russian Foreign Policy, A Council of Foreign Relations Book,* Brookings Institute, New York, 1998.

Mann, Poonam, *India's Foreign Policy in the Post Cold War Era,* Delhi, Harman Books, 2000.

Menon, K.P.S., *Indo-Soviet Treaty: Setting and Sequal,* Delhi, Vikas, 1972.

Mikoyan, S.A., "USSR and Indian Sub-continent" , *Mainstream* 8(35), May, 2, 1970.

Mishra, Girish, *Counours of Indo-Soviet Economic Co-operation,* Delhi, Allied Publishers, 1977.

Mitra, Ashok, "Friendship, Then and Now", *The Telegraph,* New Delhi, Aug. 8, 2001.

Mukherjee, Hire, *Time-Tested Treasure: Recollections and Reflections on Indo – Soviet Friendship,* Bombay, Allied Publishers, 1975.

Natchionalnoe Interesi, *Interiesi SSSR v Azi- Tioriticheskie i Prakticheskie aspectii,* Nauka, Moskva, 1991.

Naik, J.A., *Soviet Policy towards India from Stalin to Brezhnev,* Delhi, Vikas, 1970.

______________, (Ed.,) *Russia and the West: Documents: 1972-75,* New Delhi, 1982.

Neelakant, K., *Partners in Peace: A study in Indo-Soviet Relations,* Delhi, Vikas, 1972.

Nehru, Jawaharlal, *Soviet Russia: Some Random Sketches and Imressions,* Bombay, 1929.

______________, *India's Foreign Policy: Selected Speeches, September 1946 – April 1961,* Delhi, 1961.

Ollapally Deepa, "Indo-Russian strategic relations: new choices and constraints" *Journal of Strategic Studies,* Volume 25, Number 4, December 2002.

Prasad, Bimla, Ed., *Indo-Soviet Relations 1947-1972: A Documentary Study,* Allied New Delhi, 1973.

Ravindranath, N.H. and Sathaye, J., *Climate Change and Developing Countries,* Kluwer Academic Publishers, Dordrecht, Netherlands, 2002.

Remnek, Richard, B. *Soviet Policy towards India: The Role of Soviet Scholars in the Formation of Soviet Foreign Policy,* Delhi, Oxford and IBM, 1975.

Robert, Horn, *Soviet-Indian Relations: Issues and Influences,* New York, 1982.

Rothermund, Dietmar, "India and the Soviet Union", *Annals,* American Academy of political and Social Science, November, 1969.

Samra, Chattar Singh, *India and Anglo-Soviet Relations 1917-47,* (New York, 1959).

Sardesai, S.G. *India and the Russian Revolution,* New Delhi, 1967.

Sebastian, Stanislaus M., *Soviet Economic Aid to India; An analysis and evalution,* New Delhi, 1975.

Shams-ud-din (ed.) *India and Russia Towards Strategic Partnership,* Lancer's Books, New Delhi. 2002.

Sharma , Ram, "India-U.S.S.R. Relations (1947-71), From Ambivalence to Steadfastness, Part I", Monograph Discovery Publishing House, New Delhi, 1999.

Sharma, Shankar Dayal, *Studies in Indo-Soviet Cooperation,* New Delhi, 1981.

Sinha, P.B., *Indian National Liberation Movement and Russia, 1905-1917,* Unpublished Ph.D., thesis, Moscow State University, 1971.

Srivastava, Anupam, "Indo-Russian Military Technical Cooperation: Implications for Southern Asia," published in *World Affairs, Spring,* 1999.

Subrahmanaym, K., "Soviet Military Assitance", *Indo-Soviet Co-operation,* New Delhi, 1971.

Tiwari, J.C., *Basic Principles of Soviet Economic aid to India,* Aligrah, 1979.

Varma, Shanta Nedungadi, *Foreign Policy Dynamics: Moscow and India's International Conflicts,* New Delhi, Lancer's Books, 1999.

Vibhakar, Jagdish, *A Model Relationship: Twenty-five Years of Indo-Soviet Diplomatic Ties,* New Delhi, 1972.

Yakovlev, Alexander G. The Triangle of Russia-China-India: Pros and Contras in *China Report* 38:1 2002, Thousand Oaks, London, pp. 101-103.

Articles

Adomeit, Hannes, "Russia as 'great power" in World Affairs : Iimages and Reality", *International Affairs,* Vol. 71, No.1, January, 1995.

Alva, Joachim, "Indo-Soviet Relations", *Economic Times,* 21 March, 1976.

Arkhipov., I.V., "Soviet–Indian Trade and Economic Co-operation", *Link,* 15 August 1978.

Bakshi, Jyotsna, "Russia's Post-Pokhran Dilemma", *Strategic Analysis,* New Delhi, IDSA, Aug 1998.

Banerjee, Subrata, "Indo Soviet Treaty: Its Relevance Today", *Secular Democracy,* August 1980, pp. 43-48.

Bhandari, Arivnd, "Testing time for Indo-Soviet Relations", *Commerce,* December 6, 1980, pp. 1064-67.

Bhatia, Prem, "Brezhnev Visit: A Preview", *Amrita Bazar Patrika,* 7, November, 1973.

Bhatt, Anil, "Abiding Friendship", *The Hindu,* New Delhi, March 6, 2002.

Bhatia, Vinod, "Historical Ties in Surge of Liberation", *Patriot,* September 20, 1982.

_______________, "Indo – Soviet Cooperation", *Patriot,* August 9, 1983.

Blank, Stephen, and Rubinstein, Alvin Z., "Is Russia Still a Power in Asia?" *Problems of Post-Communism,* Mar-April 1997.

Brezhnev, Leonid, "No Political Dividends" *Commerce,* 20 December 1980, pp. 1151-52.

Budhraj, V.S., "India and the Soviet Union", *International Studies,* New Delhi, July-December, 1979, pp. 739-57.

______________, "The Janata Party and Indo-Soviet Relations," *Indian Journal of Political Science,* Delhi, January-March, 1976.

Chand, Attar, "India and the Soviet Union", *National Herald,* 19 June, 1976.

Chari, P.R., "Indo-Soviet Military Relations: A comment", *India Quarterly,* October-December, 1977, pp. 454-57.

Chattopadhya, Amal, "Soviet Strategy and Our foreign Policy", *Radical Humanist,* November, 1980.

Chavan, Y.B., "Indo-Soviet Cooperation Widens", *Soviet Land,* New Delhi, December 1975, p.16.

Cherian, John, A Strategic Partnership, *Frontline,* New Delhi, Vol.17, 37 issue 21, Oct.14-27, 2000.

Chenoy, Anuradha M., *India under Siege: Challenges Within and Without,* New Delhi, Wiley Eastern, 1994.

______________ "A Defining Moment", *Frontline,* Vol. 17, Issue 21, Oct. 14 27, 2000.

Conley, Jerome M., "Indo-Russian Military and Nuclear Cooperation", INSS, *Occational Paper 31,* Feb.2000.

Choudhuri, Kali Kinkar, "The Gromyko Visit," *Frontier,* 8 March, 1980, pp. 6-8.

Hewson, Robert, "Russia's PGMs Go on Show", *Jane's Defence Weekly,* October 19, 2005.

______________ "Russia Launches R-73 Upgrade", *Jane's Defence Weekly,* August 24, 2005, p.5.

Jaisingh, Hari, "Building New Strategic Ties, Moscow has Always Stood for a Strong India", *The Tribune,* New Delhi, Nov.23, 2001.

"Loyal Bear", *The Telegraph,* New Delhi, February 12, 2002.

Medvedev, Roy, Vladimir Putin, New Accents in Russia's Foreign Policy, *Rossiskaya Gazeta,* August 8, 2000.

Menon, Ramesh, Changing Contours of Indo-Russian ties, *Rediff News,* October 3, 2000.

Menon, M.S.N., Sino-Russian Treaty: Implications for India, *The Tribune,* Chandigarh, Aug. 8, 2001

Patasani, Prasanna Kumar, *India-Russia: Towards Strategic Partnership,* New Delhi, Samskriti, 2002.

Phadnis, Umashankar, "India, Russia to Sign Strategic Partnership Agreement", *Dawn,* Internet Edition, May 1, 2000.

Raghuvanshi, V. "Report urges India to widen contracting process", *Defense News,* April 30, 2001, *SIPRI Yearbook 2002.*

Raja Mohan, C., "Relocating Indo-Russian ties", *The Hindu,* New Delhi, Nov.8, 2001.

Singh, Anita Inder, 'India's Relations with Russia and Central Asia', *International Affairs,* RIIA, Vol. 71, No. 1, 1995.

Singh, V.K. "Indo-Russian Defence Co-operation and Self-Reliance: An Army View Point", *Agni,* 7 (1), May-August 2003, PP- 5-7.

Thakur, Ramesh, "Dusting off Russo-Indian Ties", *The Japan Times,* Tokyo, Monday, November 20, 2000.

Journals and News papers

New York Times.

Indian Express.

The Hindu.

"The Danger of Strategic Illusions", *The Hindu,* New Delhi, February, 2002.

"Old Friends, New Bonds", *The Hindustan Times,* New Delhi, Dec.6, 2002.

National Herald.

News Time

The Hindustan Times

The Tribune

The Kashmir Times

Daily Excelsior.

The Pioneer

Deccan Chronicle

'India to buy 320 Russian T-90 tanks', *Indian Express,* April 3, 2000.

'Indo-Russian joint declaration', *The News,* October 4, 2000.

'India settles nuclear sub lease terms with Russia', *Defence News,* October 15, 2001.

'India to hire Russian N-sub again', *Times of India,* December 20, 2000.

'Indian submarines to have missiles soon'; October 6, 2001, www.bharat-rakshak.com.

'India begins to receive Russian missiles for subs', *Defence News,* October 23, 2001.

'India Navy's sub sail from Russia', *Times of India,* August 25, 2001.

'India stretches life span of aircraft', *Defence News,* July 10, 2000.

Website Address

http://lcweb2.loc.gov/cgibin/query/r?frd/cstdy:@field(DOCID+ru0119)

http://www.imf.org/external/np/vc/2002/082602.htm.

CNN, Gennady Zyuganov candidate profile, 1996. http://edition.cnn.com/WORLD/9602/russia_zyuganov.

Daniel Treisman, "Blaming Russia First," *Foreign Affairs*, Nov/Dec. 2000. http://www.foreignaffairs.org/20001101fareviewessay946/daniel-treisman/ blaming-russia-first.html.

http://edition.cnn.com/WORLD/pivotal.elections/1996/russia/candidate.html.

http://media.washingtonpost.com/wpsrv/inatl/longterm/russiagov/stories/premier070596.htm.

http://www.pbs.org/newshour/bb/europe/july96/runoff_results1_7-4.html.

http://www.cia.gov/cia/publications/factbook/geos/rs.html.

http://www.pbs.org/newshour/bb/europe/july-dec98/russia_10-27.html

http://www.pbs.org/newshour/bb/europe/jan-june98/russia_3-23.html

http://www.cnn.com/WORLD/europe/9804/24/duma.vote.results/.

http://www.pbs.org/wgbh/commandingheights/shared/minitextlo/int_robertrubin.html#6.

'Press Release', November 6, 2002, *www.pibm.nic.in/archieve/ Ireleng.html*

http://www.pbs.org/newshour/bb/europe/july-dec98/russia_7-13.html

http://www.jamestown.org/publications_ details.php?volume_id=5&issue_id=293&article_id=3285

http://www.pbs.org/newshour/forum/september98/russia.html

http://education.guardian.co.uk/higher/comment/story/0%2C9828%2C932847%2C00.html

http://www.jamestown.org/publications_ details.php? volume_id=6&&issue_id=368

ohttp://jamestown.org/publicationsdetails. php?volume_id=2&&issue_id=21.

http://www.washtimes.com/upi-breaking/20041229-025404-5878r.htm

http://www.theglobeandmail.com/servlet/story/RTGAM.20040212.wsovi0212/BNPrint/Front.

India Looks to US for Weapons after Delay in Russian Deals", at http://www.rense.com/general19/IndialooksAL.htm.

"Indian Admiral Blasts Russian Arms Deals", at http://www.aeronautics.ru/archive/aeronews/conv/article_April_2001_10_118.htm. *India-Russia Defence Co-operation* 465.

'India, Russia to discuss LCA production', February 27, 2001, www.bharat-rakshak.com.

Index